NIKA HAZELTON'S

Pasta

COOKBOOK

NIKA HAZELTON'S

Pasta

COOKBOOK

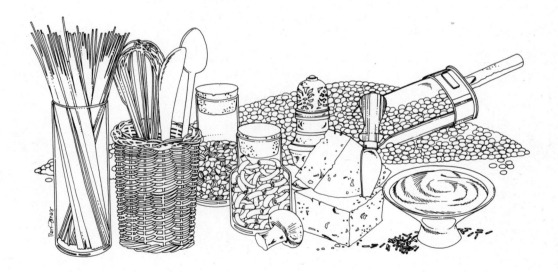

BALLANTINE BOOKS · NEW YORK

Library of Congress Catalog Card Number: 83-91170
ISBN 0-345-31511-1

Design by Beth Tondreau and Mary A. Wirth
Manufactured in the United States of America
First Edition: July 1984
10 9 8 7 6 5 4 3 2 1

For
Steven and Christina Bazerman

I am grateful to Liz Berseth, Nona Clarke, Linda Davies
and the Pasta Institute of America
for their help and assistance.

Contents

NIKA HAZELTON'S

Pasta

COOKBOOK

Introduction

This is a Pasta Cookbook for everyday cooking, featuring dishes that are appetizing, nutritious, and economical, in turns of both time and money. The book is geared toward ingredients readily found on supermarket shelves, and uses American as well as imported Italian and Oriental pastas. The book also tells you how to make pasta at home. The recipes are those that I have made and served to family and friends for years and reflect my own taste. (I wish to say here that I don't believe in spending hours and hours in the kitchen, unless it is for a special occasion.) I have not included recipes for dumplings, gnocchi, pasta rolls and other handmade farinaceous dishes because to my mind, they are not strictly pasta in the sense that spaghetti, macaroni and fettucine are. The entrees in this book are strictly limited to dishes which are invariably served on pasta or rice to carry their flavorful sauces.

The American love for pasta, which we call the large variety of products made from wheat like spaghetti, macaroni, noodles and scores of other shapes, is not one of the food fads from which our nation suffers periodically. It is based upon the solid ground that pasta can be served in infinite varieties and still constitutes economical and flavorful nutrition. Pasta is a meal maker in itself. The simplest pasta dish satisfies the appetite and palate in a unique manner, appealing even to difficult eaters like children and meat-and-potatoes-only addicts. Pasta has staying power and its taste can be varied at will with costly or meager amounts of condiments or leftovers. And pasta makes excellent vegetarian meals.

Pasta gives you choices. For special events, you can spend hours making your own unstuffed or stuffed pastas, but you can also make wonderful dishes quickly with store-bought dry pasta.

Besides a big pot filled with boiling water and a strainer, no equipment is needed to cook pasta; even homemade pasta does not require any special tools besides a rolling pin.

WHAT IS PASTA?

Pasta is made with flour, water and sometimes eggs; vegetable purees and other flavors such as curry or sesame may be added as well. Its origins are obscure but it appears that the Romans, great consumers of wheat products, knew it in some shape or other. Stories about Marco Polo bringing pasta back from China are pure legend; all he is reputed to say is that in China they have pasta resembling the Italian product. As for America, Thomas Jefferson is said to have brought it back from his European travels.

The fact is that pasta is a universal, ubiquitous product that came into being wherever people had to invent uses for the foodstuffs they had at hand: Hence subvarieties such as Oriental soy and rice pastas.

Western pasta is made with water and hard durum winter wheat flour, which is rich in gluten and "stronger" than ordinary flour; it makes pasta that will not come apart in boiling water and lends itself to diverse shapes. *Semola* is fine pasta flour milled from durum wheat; *semolina* (or *semolino*) is one of the coarser grinds of this flour, which in Italy may be bought in different grinds from fine to coarse. *Semolina flour* also makes the best kind of pasta at home, but be sure not to ask simply for "semolina," which is the product known commercially as Cream of Wheat; rather one should always ask for SEMOLINA *FLOUR* FOR PASTA MAKING.

A modern pasta plant may be almost completely automated, with electric control panels used to direct the operations. In such a plant the semolina, farina and/or other high quality hard wheat flour is purchased in bulk and arrives by rail in airslide cars. A pneumatic unloading system transfers it to bulk storage bins, which automatically stop the loading when they are full. Another pneumatic transfer system moves the flour to press bins for mixing with water. The dough is kneaded, then forced by presses through dies, which are metal discs with holes. The size and shape of the holes determine what the finished product will be. Round or oval holes, varying from $\frac{1}{32}$ to $\frac{5}{64}$ of an inch, produce the solid rods which are fedelini, linguine and other forms of spaghetti. When steel pins are placed in the holes of the die, the extruded dough is tubular and is called macaroni. If the pin has a notch on one side, the dough passes through one side of the hole of the die faster than it does the other; the result is a slightly curved product such as the familiar elbow macaroni. A revolving knife attached to the die cuts the dough at frequent intervals into short lengths. Dies are available for making at least 325 shapes of pasta. Even more variety is possible by cutting the extruded dough into different lengths.

The pasta is automatically conveyed into drying units. Long goods, such as spaghetti and long macaroni, are hung on rods. Elbow macaroni, other short goods and special shapes are spread on belts; the product is dropped from level to level, being reduced in moisture on each level as it passes.

Usually a product goes through a preliminary dryer and a finishing dryer. Drying is a critical part of the manufacture of pasta. The heat and moisture of the air and the length of time in the dryer must be determined accurately for each product. If drying is too fast, the pasta will check and break easily; if drying is too slow, it can spoil.

Egg noodles are mixed in much the same way as macaroni and spaghetti, but with the addition of 5.5 percent egg solids (fresh, powdered or frozen) as required by law. The shaping of noodles is accomplished by pressing between rollers to form thin sheets which are then cut to the desired widths. Drying follows a procedure similar to that for other pasta products.

For the most part, packaging of the finished pasta products is accomplished by machine. The many continuously moving parts of the assembly lines supply boxes, open them and move them into position to receive pasta which has been weighed automatically. Product and packages may move from the beginning of the line to the end throughout the whole process without human assistance. Some few special products, however, such as lasagne, may still require hand packing.

Packaged products usually travel by conveyor belt to a storage area. Here, as in the rest of the plant, equipment and layout are designed for easy cleaning; sanitation is all-important in a food production plant.

In Italy the law requires that only pure durum wheat flour and water may be used in making pasta; no artificial coloring or preservatives may be added. Colored pastas may only be made with natural vegetable colors and Italian egg pasta, and by law must contain at least 5 whole eggs for every two pounds of flour.

Commercial American pastas are made with flours that have been more refined in milling than Italian ones, and are fortified with vitamins. Colored American pastas are usually made with powdered dehydrated vegetables, and commercial American egg pastas with frozen eggs and egg solids.

According to the American Pasta Institute, pasta sales in the U.S. break down as follows:

long or spaghetti-type pastas	40%
elbow macaroni	30%
egg noodles	20%
assorted shapes	10%

And according to Time magazine of April 26, 1982, Americans in 1981 ate about 2 billion pounds of pasta, or about 9 pounds per person a year. (Italians are the biggest pasta eaters, with about 60 pounds per person a year.) Since then American pasta consumption has increased, and we are getting right up front in our pasta avalanche: In May 1983, Americans ate 1½ billion pounds of dry commercial pasta, or about 6½ pounds per capita. It seems a lot, but then not compared to the Italians' 60 pounds per person per year!

NUTRITIONAL VALUE

Here are some details on nutrition for the majority of domestic and imported pasta products:

Protein

Pasta products are valuable providers of protein. They have a good distribution of the essential amino acids which are necessary for optimum health and growth in humans. These are: threonine, isoleucine, leucine, methionine, phenylalanine and valine. Pasta products also contain some lysine and tryptophan. Analysis of pasta products shows the following:

	PROTEIN CONTENT
Macaroni and Spaghetti	12.5% to 13%
Egg noodles	13% to 13.5%

Carbohydrates

Through their complex carbohydrate content, pasta products supply high energy for growth and activity. The caloric content of two ounces *uncooked* pasta products is:

	CALORIES
Macaroni	210
Spaghetti	210
Egg noodles	220

To put it plainly, it is not the pasta that will fatten you, but what you put on it in the way of dressing and saucing the dish.

Sodium

Pasta products are low sodium foods. Analysis of two ounces *uncooked* pasta shows the average sodium content to be:

Macaroni and Spaghetti	0.60 mg.
Egg noodles	1.80 mg.

Fat

Pasta products are also low fat foods. Average fat content:

Macaroni and Spaghetti	1.4%
Egg noodles	4.5%

Digestibility

Pasta products are digested at a moderate rate and provide not only energy, but satiety which prevents the return of hunger too soon after a meal. They are suitable for the normal diet from childhood to old age. Nutritionists determine the coefficient of digestibility from the relation between nutrients in food consumed and nutrients excreted. Pasta products are highly digestible, as shown by the following:

NUTRIENT IN PASTA PRODUCTS	COEFFICIENT OF DIGESTIBILITY
Carbohydrates	98%
Protein	85%
Fat	90%

DRY PASTA CUTS

There are literally scores of names for different pasta cuts, depending on the manufacturer's fancy and on the region of Italy from which they stem. Italy is a country that is greatly attached to its own regional traditions, including the culinary terms for some things. For instance, fettucine and agnolotti in Rome become tagliatelle and ravioli in Bologna. The learned Dr. Mario Pei, professor of Romance Philology at New York's Columbia University, once made up a list of Italian pasta names, which came to no less than 106:

ITALIAN NAMES	LIBERAL TRANSLATION
Acini di pepe	peppercorns
Alpini	Alpines
Amorini	little loves, Cupids

ITALIAN NAMES	LIBERAL TRANSLATION
Anelli	rings
Anellini	little rings, ringlets
Anellini rigati	grooved rings
Arancini	little oranges
Assabesi	no translation
Bavettini	remnant in the steel industry
Bocconcini	little mouthfuls
Bucatini	little holed ones
Cannelle	little reeds
Cannellini	very small reeds
Cannelloni	big reeds
Cannoni	cannons
Capellini	little hairs
Cappelli di prete	Priests' hats
Cappelli Pagliaccio	clown's hats
Cavatelli	no translation (maybe little twists)
Conchiglie	shells
Conchigliette	little shells
Creste Gallo	coxcombs
Datteri	dates
Di Natale	of Christmas
Di Natale rigati	grooved Christmas ones
Ditali	thimbles
Ditalini	small thimbles
Elene	named after Queen of Italy
Elettrici rigati	grooved electric ones
Farfalle	butterflies
Farfallette	small butterflies
Farfalloni	big butterflies
Favoriti	favorites
Fedelini	little faithful ones

Fettuce	ribbons	Parigine	Parisians
Fettuccelle	small ribbons	Pastina	little dough
Fettucce Riccie	curly ribbons	Penne	pens or feathers
Fiorentini	Florentines	Pennine	pen nibs
Foratini	little holed ones	Perciatelli	no translation
Foratini fini	fine little holed ones	Quadrettini	little squares
Funghini	little mushrooms	Reginini	little queens
Fusilli	spindles	Rex	king
Fusilli bucati	holed spindles	Ricciolini	little curls
Gnocchi	dumplings	Rigatoni	big grooved ones
Lancette	little spears	Risino	little rice
Lasagne	pots	Rita	girl's name
Lasagne riccie	curled pots	Rosa Marina	sea rose
Lingue di passero	sparrows' tongues	Rotelle	little wheels
Linguine	little tongues	Rotini	little wheels
Linguine fine	fine little tongues	Scungilli	shellfish similar to scallops
Lumache	snails	Semi Melone	melon seeds
Lumachine	small snails	Spaghetti	little pieces of cord
Lumacone	big snails	Spaghettini	little spaghetti
Maccaroncelli	medium small macaroni	Spiedini	little skewers
Mafalda	name of Princess	Stelle	stars
Magliette	links	Stellini	little stars
Magliette spaccate	split links	Stivaletti	little boots
Margherita	daisy	Stortini	little twisted ones
Maruzze	seashell	Tagliatelle	little cut ones
Messani	mediums	Tirolesi	Tyroleans
Mezzanelli	small mediums	Tortellini	little twisted ones
Millefiori	thousand flowers	Triangoli	triangles
Mille Righe	thousand stripes or grooves	Tripolini	named after Tripoli
		Tubetti	little tubes
Mostaccioli	little mustaches	Tubettini	extra small tubes
Napoleoni	Napoleons	Tufini	porous rock or joint swelling
Occhi di lupo	wolf's eyes		
Ondulati	wavy ones	Tufoli	same as tufini
Orzo	barley	Vongolette	little clams
Panierini	little baskets	Vermicelli	little worms

Ziti	dialect for bridegrooms
Ziti tagliati	sawed-off bridegrooms
Zitoni	big bridegrooms

Note that many of these pastas come in different sizes, each specifically so named. But pasta is not limited to the Western world. China, Japan and the Far East also dote on the product, which you will find in Chinese and Oriental markets.

ORIENTAL PASTA

To the surprise of many Italians and Americans a lot of pasta is eaten in the Orient, largely in soups. The reasons for this popularity is the same as in the U.S.—pasta tastes good, is nourishing, goes far and is inexpensive.

In spite of specific names of origin (Chinese noodles, etc.) the dried noodles we buy here in America are the product of many Oriental countries, such as China, Malaysia, Thailand, Hong Kong and even Japan, though Japanese noodles are different. The most popular of these noodles are briefly described as follows:

EGG NOODLES can be bought fresh, dried or frozen in Oriental markets. They're made from wheat flour, water and eggs like any noodles, and like any noodles, they are easy to overcook; they cook in minutes and the thinnest ones, in seconds. It is best to cook the noodles separately before adding them to soup or other dishes.

Some cooks advocate soaking them in warm water before cooking; I don't think this is necessary. A tablespoon or less of cooking oil added to the boiling water in which the noodles will cook prevents them from sticking together, since they are very soft. If you can't find Chinese noodles, as egg noodles are frequently called, use linguine for an acceptable substitute.

CELLOPHANE NOODLES, also known as Bean Thread noodles, Silver Threads or Shining noodles, are, to my mind, more interesting than the noodles mentioned above. They are made from the starch of the mung bean. These noodles should be soaked in hot water for 15–30 minutes, drained and then cooked briefly or until tender in boiling water or soup.

RICE NOODLES are made from rice flour, should be soaked in cold water first from 15 minutes to 1 hour then cooked briefly in boiling water or soup until tender. They come in different widths.

RICE STICK NOODLES, also made from rice, are very thin threads sold dry. They cook in seconds or at best, minutes, in boiling water or soup. For dishes other than soups, cook the noodles, drain them well and mix them with the other ingredients of your dish.

JAPANESE NOODLES. When called Udon, they are thick, whole wheat noodles usually served in broth. When called Somen, they are thinner and used in cold dishes and also in soups. Soba, very popular noodles, are made from buckwheat flour and often served cold in salads.

What it all comes down to is that people make noodles or pasta whenever they have a suitable starch, be it in the East or the West.

Personally, I like the slippery Cellophane noodles because they are different. I also think—and may cooking purists forgive me as I dodge their brickbats—that for the likes of most of us, there is not such a lot of difference between the Cellophane and Rice noodles. I can only repeat what I feel about All pasta—use it as you wish, interchange it, be strictly ethnic or do what you wish, and it is certain to taste good *when it is not overcooked*.

Since it is impossible to describe all these pastas in this book, I will limit myself to classifying them into two large main categories: Short Pastas and Long Pastas. To the Short Pasta family belong plain or grooved penne, wheels, shells, rigatoni, bows, coxcombs, elbows, ditali, mostaccioli, tubetti, bow ties, orzo and the little soup pastas like alphabets and tiny rings.

To the Long Pasta family belong string-like products like spaghetti, capellini and vermicelli; those that are hollow on the inside like macaroni, ziti and bucatini; those which are flat like tagliatelle and linguine; those shaped like ribbons, which may or may not be curly at one or both sides like lasagne and mafalde, plain or riccie (curled); and the long pasta twists called fusilli, though there are also short fusilli.

———   · · ·   ———

HOW TO USE PASTA

The beauty of pasta is that there are several shapes for every kind of recipe you can name. It is entirely possible to interchange shapes, so long as the exchange is made among products of similar size and shape and so long as the cooked volume is about the same. Here are some of the best ways of using pasta.

ELBOW MACARONI, SHELLS, CORKSCREW MACARONI, BOWS AND OTHER SHAPES OF SIMILAR SIZE:

Casseroles (meat, fish, poultry, cheese, vegetable)
Salads
Soups and stews

SPAGHETTI OF VARIOUS SIZES, FUSILLI (TWISTED SPAGHETTI), LINGUINE (FLAT SPAGHETTI):

With sauces, meat, poultry, vegetables, fish or cheese
Simple dishes with butter or oil, herbs, grated cheese

EGG NOODLES (FINE, MEDIUM OR WIDE):

Casseroles
With sauces
Simple side dishes
Soups
Noodle puddings

PASTINA, AND OTHER VERY SMALL SHAPES

Soups
Children's meals

STORE-BOUGHT DRY PASTA OR FRESH HOMEMADE?

There is no reason why you can't enjoy both kinds of pasta—though admittedly, not both at the same time! All pasta sauces can be used on fresh homemade as well as on purchased dry pasta.

The main difference in preparing the two kinds lies in their cooking time. Fresh homemade pasta is done in a matter of minutes (and in some cases even less) and therefore has to be carefully watched or it will be mushy or disintegrate. Also, the yield of fresh homemade pasta is smaller than that of the dry commercial product because the homemade variety has greater moisture content, absorbs less water in cooking, and therefore swells up less. Twelve to fourteen ounces of homemade noodles will yield about 4 cups cooked.

The advantages of store-bought pasta are that it is inexpensive and easy to buy in a variety of shapes, and that it is ready to use when you need it quickly. Dry pasta also keeps well, though not indefinitely—it *will* go stale. Personally, I cannot find any disadvantages to good-quality dry pasta. On the contrary, I, as so many other pasta lovers, much prefer a good dry pasta to most homemade pastas.

Unless pasta made at home is prepared with the proper flour and enough time to spend on making it correctly, it is infinitely better to use dry pasta. Making good pasta at home is an art, even today with the help of machines. It takes time and a certain amount of practice to be pasta perfect, as with pastry making and other specialized kinds of cooking. Good homemade pasta is a great treat, and in Italy, the pasta paradise par excellence, it is only made for special occasions. No Italian cook makes pasta for the fun of it as so many Americans do now that homemade pasta has become fashionable. Homemade pasta is treated seriously in Italy. Restaurants advertise it as such and guests feel honored when served it. It takes time to make homemade pasta, from clearing the kitchen and preparing the surfaces, to finding clean cloths for drying it. What it comes down to—the choice of pasta is yours and yours alone.

Bought Freshly Made Pasta

During the last few years many shops have begun to make and sell their own fresh pasta with fettucine, ravioli and tortellini the most popular varieties. These pastas are generally very good, though expensive, and provide a change in the diet without much effort beyond paying. If you want odd, fancy pastas, you are likely to find them in these specialty shops. Personally, I don't like them.

Pasta of this kind is best used when freshly made. However, it can be bagged in plastic and refrigerated for a couple of days, or frozen for a couple of weeks. Do not keep or freeze it any longer, because the pasta will dry out and lose flavor.

LONG PASTA

LINGUINE

SPAGHETTI

BUCATINI

CAPELLINI

LONG FUSILLI

LASAGNE

TAGLIATELLE

ZITI

MACARONI

MAFALDE

SHORT PASTA

SHELLS

PENNE, GROOVED AND PLAIN

ORZO

DITALI

WHEELS

RIGATONI

SOUP PASTAS

ELBOWS

MOSTACCIOLI

BOWS AND BOW TIES

SHORT FUSILLI

TUBETTI

Domestic or Imported?

The major brands of domestic pasta are excellent and so are many of the minor ones. They vary slightly as to chewiness, yield and flavor, but even my Italian mother had to admit that domestic pasta beat all but the best brands of imported pasta.

In our diet conscious age, some producers, both domestic and foreign, have come out with so-called lower calorie or diet pastas. Personally I find that the caloric difference is not great enough to matter and also, I think white pasta more appetizing than the dark-hued varieties.

PASTA–MAKING ACCESSORIES

The current all-American pasta passion has produced a large number of accessories, such as ravioli crimpers, rollers and shaped trays, drying machines, complicated cheese graters, tomato presses, manual and electric pasta machines, electric mixer and food processor pasta-making attachments and all-in-one-step electric pasta extruders where the raw pasta ingredients go in at one end and come out in the desired shape at the other. Before a brief discussion of their relative merits it is *most important* to ask yourself the question of how often you would use any of these objects. Experience has shown that, car-

ried away by their first enthusiasm for easier homemade pasta, people will invest (often quite a lot of money) in a special machine, use it a dozen times and then put it away. In my opinion, it is not wise to spend a sizeable sum on any kitchen or other gadget that will not be frequently used.

Pasta Machines

All pasta machines, manual or electric, come with accurate instructions on how to use, clean and maintain them. Almost always, instructions include the formula for the basic dough best suited to that particular machine. IT IS MOST IMPORTANT TO FOLLOW THE INSTRUCTIONS, ESPECIALLY THOSE FOR HOW TO USE AND CLEAN THE MACHINES. I have also found that the dough formula given in the instructions of a given machine works best for that machine.

Making the dough

This is not difficult (see pages 119–23) but it requires some thought and effort to do it properly by hand. You can also make a satisfactory dough in a food processor or, in larger quantities, an electric mixer with a dough hook.

———   • • •   ———

Kneading the dough

By hand this requires some effort, strength and persistence to get the dough smooth and silky, but the results are superior to machine kneading.

Rolling the dough

Machines that roll the dough will also knead it further in the process of rolling it. For ordinary household use, a manual or electric Italian pasta machine is the most useful (manual machines are not expensive). Be sure to secure the machine to a heavy table or counter for greatest stability, and do not overload or force it. To avoid overloading, divide the dough into workable portions. Always start by rolling the dough through the widest (most open) position, and always lower the setting one notch at a time. Crank firmly but gently; if the machine shows some resistance, remove the piece of dough and make it smaller.

Cuisinart, the popular food processor, has a separate pasta rolling and cutting attachment which is fastened to the original machine after the dough has been made. The advantage of this is that you have the Cuisinart for your general use and the pasta attachment for your special purpose. But I find that the pasta is not as satisfactory as that from a dough made and kneaded by hand and rolled by a conventional roller.

Home size one step pasta extruding machines (commercial dry pasta is made by this process) are now available from a number of manufacturers such as Simac. With these machines, as with the Cuisinart, you *must* follow the manufacturer's directions for the dough formula, which may be a little different from those for hand-made pastas. These machines are certainly easy and convenient, but again I find that homemade pasta done in a more conventional method is preferable—if only because it is better kneaded.

Always follow instructions for keeping your machine scrupulously clean. This is not always the easiest thing, especially with the automatic kinds. *Never, but never* put water on any of the machines or their parts, not even with a damp rag.

HOW MUCH DRY PASTA TO BUY

Dry pasta products keep well, and it is practical to buy several packages at a time. Ideally one would have enough macaroni, spaghetti and egg noodles on hand to provide for several meals. The convenience and short cooking time of pasta products makes them good insurance for emergency meals and for busy-day cooking. Prices do not fluctuate as they do with many other foods, and therefore there is no need to watch for special sales; pasta is always a bargain.

HOW MUCH DRY PASTA TO COOK

When a pasta product is used for a main dish, a good rule of thumb is to allow two ounces uncooked product per person. However, one has to consider the appetites of the various members of the family. For many, 4 ounces of spaghetti is the logical amount for one serving. It may be helpful to know that macaroni and spaghetti approximately double in volume after cooking, while egg noodles remain about the same.

The following table will be helpful in determining the right amount to cook when one type is substituted for another, and in deciding how much will be needed for any given number of persons. Eight ounces will usually provide about four servings.

PRODUCT	DRY	COOKED
Elbow macaroni	2 cups (8 ounces)	4½ cups (approx.)
Spaghetti	8 ounces	5 cups (approx.)
Egg noodles	8 ounces (about 4 cups)	4 cups (approx.)

——— • • • ———

ABOUT PASTA SAUCES HOW MUCH SAUCE TO MAKE

The best sauce for your pasta dish is the one that tastes best to you. Let your taste, budget, and availability of sauce-fixings—in short, your creativity—inspire your pasta meals. One day it may be a rich sauce, the other a simple dressing of herbed butter and grated cheese.

ABOUT THE AMOUNT OF SAUCE TO USE: This cannot be answered unequivocally since it depends on individual taste and the kind of sauce. Italians like little sauce on their pasta whereas most Americans like a larger amount of sauce. To help you with a dilemma that only you can solve, **I have presented the yield of the sauces in cups rather than servings. I figure on 1 cup sauce for every four ounces of dry pasta, but you take it from here. Saucing is a matter of personal taste. However, remember that piquant sauces with anchovies or oil-garlic sauces should be used more sparingly than mild sauces.**

It is well to keep in mind a few rules that will make your pasta dishes taste as they should. With short pastas, especially grooved and hollow ones, use a sauce with bits of meat, fish or vegetables which will cling to and penetrate the ridges and hollows. Also suited to these pastas are "white" sauces made with butter, cream and sometimes flour. For long or hollowed long pastas like spaghetti, linguine or fettucine, tomato sauces of every kind are good as are simple condiments like oil and garlic, or seafood with or without tomatoes.

Remember that a heavy pasta, whatever the kind, takes a heavy sauce; I am thinking of rigatoni or wheels or lasagne. Thin, small or fragile pasta is best with simple dressings like butter and cheese. To my mind, noodles are the best kind of pasta side dish. However, in the end, it is your own taste that will dictate what sauce or dressing for which kind of pasta.

INGREDIENTS

Tomatoes

Since so many sauces are based on tomatoes, all I can say is that fresh, ripe, flavorful tomatoes such as we get in the height of summer taste best. But rather than using the pallid, pitiful and tasteless tomatoes found at other times of the year, use canned tomatoes in your cooking as the Italians do. But buy the best possible grade of canned tomatoes, preferably Italian-style or imported plum tomatoes. Inexpensive canned tomatoes are thin bodied and watery, and a waste of other ingredients. However, I have successfully used 28-ounce cans of tomato hunks. If you should have to drain the tomatoes, do this by placing them in *one* layer in a colander. Do not pile them up, because only one layer will drain properly. Reserve the drained-off tomato liquid for other uses. In any case remember that tomatoes, whether drained or fresh, vary in liquid content, and adjust your recipe accordingly by either reducing the excess liquid or, if too dry, adding some of the drained-off liquid to the dish *a little at a time*.

Tomato paste

The imported pastes are more flavorful than domestic ones, though these will certainly serve the purpose. If you don't use up a whole can, transfer the remaining paste into a clean container and freeze, or dribble a little olive oil over the top, close tightly and refrigerate.

Cheese

With a very few exceptions, such as pasta served with an oil/anchovy sauce or other fish sauces, pasta in Italy is invariably served with grated Parmesan or Pecorino cheese. The imported Parmesan, known as Parmigiano Reggiano, is the very finest and worth every penny of its rather high cost. It is straw colored, crumbly rather than dry, and must by law be aged for at least two years. The genuine article is distinguished by its rind, with the words Parmigiano Reggiano in pin-prick-like script. Parmigiano Reggiano is also part of the Italian cheese tray because it is so delicious to nibble. Lesser imported Parmesans such as grana are not quite as wonderful, but they cost less and will also serve.

Keep the cheese well wrapped in a layer of waxed paper and one of aluminum foil and refrigerate.

The same goes for Pecorino, sheep's milk cheese which is made all over Italy to be eaten fresh or dried. The two main varieties used for grating in the United States are Pecorino Sardo, a milder, somewhat crumbly cheese, and Pecorino Romano, which is more pungent; this is the cheese commonly known as Romano. Both kinds are imported from Italy and can be found in cheese stores. The Romano sold in supermarkets in a triangle shape will serve if you can't get the real thing.

Important: Whichever cheese you use should be freshly grated. If you must buy domestic Parmesan or Romano, buy it in hunks rather than grated. Bottled grated cheese is apt to be stale, rather flavorless and full of additives for a long shelf life.

Olive Oil

The best olive oil, known as *extra vergine*, is produced by the first of three pressings. It is low in acidity and contains no additives. It is very expensive, but it will make all the difference in the flavor of a dish. Tuscan and Ligurian olive oils and those from north of Rome are lighter and very fragrant. South of Rome and in Sicily the olive oil is much heavier. Again, it is all a matter of personal taste. However, there are much less expensive olive oils like Berio and

Bertolli, found in supermarkets, which will serve well. As olive oil is essential to Italian pasta dishes, peanut and/or sesame and/or chili oil are necessary for Oriental pasta dishes. Peanut oil is found in all supermarkets, the others in Oriental groceries.

Pancetta

Pancetta is used in Italian cooking as we use bacon. It comes from the same part of the hog as bacon, but is salami shaped and is cured totally differently with salt and spices. It makes an Italian pasta dish more flavorful than bacon, but bacon or blanched salt pork can be substituted since only Italian groceries and specialty stores sell pancetta. Always buy pancetta in about ½-inch-thick slices because in big hunks it is hard to cut up. Frozen it keeps indefinitely and the frozen slices thaw very quickly.

Prosciutto

Prosciutto stands for any kind of ham in Italy, whereas to us prosciutto is cured, uncooked ham (*prosciutto crudo* in Italy). This prosciutto is much more flavorful than cooked ham. Due to import restrictions, prosciutto cannot be imported into the United States. But several kinds of Italian-style prosciuttos are now produced in the United States. Sliced, any prosciutto dries out quickly so it is well to buy only small quantities at a time.

Acceptable substitutes for prosciutto in cooking are Westphalian ham, American country hams, smoked hams and Canadian bacon. Naturally, the flavor of a dish will vary depending on the variety of ham used. If very salty, the prosciutto or substitute should be blanched in boiling water for two to three minutes and then patted dry.

TIPS FOR SERVING PASTA

All pasta should be served in heated serving dishes and heated plates. Shallow bowls and regular soup plates, thanks to their shapes that make for easy mounding of the food, are good for serving pasta. Pasta should be served on plates or bowls large enough to make tossing the dish with the sauce possible.

Regardless of the kind of sauce used, it must be ready when the pasta is cooked. Pasta that stands waiting for its sauce gets gummy and unattractive. To my mind a reheated sauced pasta dish is not worth eating.

Sauce mixes better with pasta if you ladle half of the sauce into a serving dish, top it with pasta, and top the pasta with the remaining sauce. If you serve individual dishes with pasta, place the pasta on the plate and top it with the sauce—as in Italian restaurants.

Some cooks stir two tablespoons soft butter into one pound of pasta for a richer taste before adding the sauce. Other cooks stir one to two tablespoons butter into their sauce, especially into tomato sauces. A plain tomato sauce also benefits from two to three tablespoons heavy cream.

Basic Directions for Cooking Dry Pasta

YIELD: 4 MEDIUM SERVINGS

2 cups (8 ounces) dry pasta
3 quarts water
1 tbs salt*

When larger amounts are prepared, add 4 to 6 quarts of water and 2 tablespoons of salt for each additional pound of pasta.**

In a large pot, heat water to the boiling point.

A big soup pot, kettle or Dutch oven is needed for cooking pasta. It should not be too heavy or it will be difficult to drain off the water into a colander after cooking.

Gradually add salt, then pasta. With spaghetti, grasp a handful and place one end of the strands in the water; as it softens gently push the pasta into the water until all of it is submerged. Be sure the water continues to boil. The rapid and continuous boiling helps to keep the pasta moving about so it will cook quickly, evenly and without sticking together.

Cook, uncovered, stirring frequently with a long fork or wooden spoon until tender. Stirring helps to keep the pasta evenly distributed and moving in the boiling water so that all of it will be cooked at the same time.

Test for doneness by tasting a piece of pasta. It should be tender, yet firm—al dente, "to the tooth." Cooking time will vary with the size and thickness of the product used. Very small pasta may cook in 2 minutes while some large shapes may require 15; average is 8 to 10 minutes. Cook for a little shorter time if the pasta will be used in a casserole and receive further cooking.

Immediately drain the pasta in a colander. Serve as quickly as possible, or mix with other ingredients in the recipe, for freshly cooked pasta is the very best kind there is. Do *not* rinse unless the pasta is to be used in a cold salad. Then, rinse with cold water and drain again.

Overcooking is the worst and most common of crimes against pasta, as is not cooking it in enough *rapidly boiling* water. Generally speaking, package directions advise too long a cooking time; ignore them and taste the pasta as it cooks, and drain it while still al dente or to your liking. Shake the cooked pasta not quite totally dry for the butter or sauce to cling all the better to it.

*Salting the water in which pasta is cooked is traditional and unquestionably adds to the taste of the cooked product. However, the salt may be reduced from 1 tablespoon to 2 teaspoons or even 1, and if for dietary necessity you can't have any salt in your food at all, omit it.

**Some cooks advocate adding a tablespoon or so of oil to the cooking water to prevent the pasta from sticking together. The Italians rarely do this, but I admit that it helps and I urge it for cooking large pastas such as giant shells or lasagne.

Appetizers, Soups and Stews

Easy Pasta Shell Appetizers

Postada

Chinese and Fresh Mushroom Soup

East Oriental-Style Soup with Noodles

Lobster or Shrimp Stew Over Thin Egg Noodles

Nona's Ceylon Coconut Soup

Nona's Curried Soup with Bean Threads

Oyster Stew

Pork and Cardamon Stew for Thin Spaghetti

Quick Madeira or Sherry Stew

Simple Oriental Soup with Noodles

Sturdy Country Vegetable Stew

Thick Pasta and Bean Soup

Easy Pasta Shell Appetizers

3 TO 4 SERVINGS

2 ounces (about 1 cup) large dry pasta shells
1 box (5 ounces) Boursin cheese with garlic
    and herbs
Parsley sprigs (optional)

Fill large heavy saucepan ⅔ to ¾ full of water and bring to boiling point. Add 2 teaspoons salt and the pasta shells. Return to boil and cook 12 to 15 minutes or until shells are al dente, stirring once or twice. Drain. Rinse with cold water and drain well. Using a knife, stuff each pasta shell with a scant teaspoon of cheese. If desired, garnish each appetizer with a very small sprig or part of a sprig of parsley.

Postada

A friend brought this very peppery and easy pasta novelty from Texas, where it was served to her with drinks. It *must* be well chilled and thinly sliced, to be eaten as is or with a topping or dipping sauce. I was charmed with finding something truly original in pasta dishes.

8 TO 12 SERVINGS

1 tablespoon salt
1 pound regular size spaghetti
8 eggs
1 cup finely diced ham
⅔ cup freshly grated Parmesan cheese
⅓ cup butter, melted
2 tablespoons freshly ground black pepper or
    to taste
4 teaspoons sugar

Bring a large pot of water to boiling point. Add 1 tablespoon salt and the spaghetti and return to boil. Cook until spaghetti is firm to the bite (al dente), about 8 to 10 minutes (time will vary depending on brand of spaghetti). Drain in colander. In the same large pot beat eggs with a whisk or rotary beater until well blended. Stir in ham, cheese, butter, pepper and sugar; mix well. Add drained spaghetti and mix until evenly coated with egg mixture. Turn into a buttered 12-cup bundt pan. Bake in preheated 350°F oven until the top is lightly browned and mixture is set, about 45 minutes. Remove from oven; let stand 5 minutes. Loosen edges with knife and invert onto a plate or platter. Let cool, then chill well. Cut in thin slices and serve as an appetizer or hors d'oeuvre.

• • •

CHINESE AND FRESH MUSHROOM SOUP

My adaptation of a multi-multi-ingredient soup. I use transparent cellophane noodles in this dish, but thin egg noodles (Chinese or American) or very thin spaghetti would also serve. Cook noodles according to package direction, but very much al dente.

4 SERVINGS

- 2 ounces dried Chinese mushrooms
- 2 ounces transparent cellophane noodles (bean threads)
- 4 to 5 cups chicken bouillon
- 1½ tablespoons soy sauce
- 8 ounces fresh mushrooms, thinly sliced
- 2 green onions, white and green parts, thinly sliced
- ½ teaspoon hot sesame or chili oil or to taste

Salt
Freshly ground pepper
2 tablespoons dry Sherry (optional)

Soak mushrooms in warm water to cover for 15 minutes. Drain, remove tough stems and slice thinly. Soak cellophane noodles in plenty of warm water for 20 minutes or until very soft and transparent. Drain and cut into 2-inch pieces. Heat the bouillon in a large saucepan. Add the dried mushrooms and soy sauce, cover and simmer over medium heat for 5 minutes. Add the fresh mushrooms, green onions and oil and simmer for 5 more minutes. Add the noodles. Check the seasoning, adding salt and pepper to taste. Simmer for 3 to 5 more minutes or until soup is heated through. Remove from heat, stir in the Sherry and serve immediately.

Note: Cellophane noodles tend to drop to the bottom of the soup. Make sure to include some in each serving.

EASY ORIENTAL-STYLE SOUP WITH NOODLES

4 TO 6 SERVINGS

4 cups chicken broth
8 ounces mushrooms, sliced
½ cup julienne-cut carrot (1 × ⅛ inch)—about
    1 medium carrot
½ cup julienne-cut water chestnuts (purchase
    canned whole water chestnuts, drain and cut
    into ¼-inch strips)
¼ cup diagonally sliced green onions with part
    tops (about 4 medium)
1 tablespoon soy sauce
1 teaspoon ground ginger
2 ounces cellophane noodles (bean threads),
    very thin spaghetti or fine egg noodles
1 medium whole boned skinned chicken
    breast (about 8 ounces), halved, trimmed of
    fat and cut into 1 × ¼-inch strips
2 cups washed fresh spinach leaves, torn into
    bite-size pieces

In large saucepan combine chicken broth, mushrooms, carrot, water chestnuts, green onions, soy sauce and ginger. Bring to boiling point. Add noodles and simmer 5 minutes, or until noodles are al dente, stirring once or twice. With kitchen shears cut cellophane noodles or spaghetti into 3- to 4-inch lengths. Add chicken. Reduce heat and simmer uncovered 3 to 5 minutes or until chicken is tender. Add spinach and cook about 1 minute or just until spinach wilts. Ladle into soup bowls and serve hot.

• • •

LOBSTER OR SHRIMP STEW OVER THIN EGG NOODLES

Never boil this stew, but only simmer it; cook the noodles al dente.

2 TO 3 SERVINGS

½ cup (1 stick) butter
1 pound cooked lobster meat, flaked or
    cooked shelled shrimp
4 cups milk
2 cups heavy cream
Salt
Freshly ground pepper
Cayenne pepper or hot pepper sauce to taste
    (optional)
½ teaspoon sweet paprika
4 to 6 ounces thin egg noodles, fresh cooked al
    dente and drained

Melt the butter in a saucepan large enough to contain all the ingredients. Add the lobster or shrimp and cook over medium heat, stirring constantly, for about 3 minutes. Remove from heat and cover the saucepan. In another saucepan, combine milk and cream and scald, but do not boil. Pour over the lobster or shrimp. Season with salt, pepper and cayenne and paprika.

Cool, then cover and refrigerate for 2 to 3 hours or overnight for best flavor (or serve immediately).

At serving time, turn stew into double boiler top and heat over boiling water just until heated through. Divide the cooked pasta between 2 or 3 bowls and pour the hot lobster or shrimp stew over pasta. Serve at once, very hot.

NONA'S CEYLON COCONUT SOUP

4 TO 6 SERVINGS

1 medium-size fresh coconut*
½ cup milk
2 cups water
3 tablespoons butter
1 large onion, minced (1 cup)
1 cup diagonally sliced celery (2 to 3 ribs)
2 cups chicken broth
2 ounces cellophane noodles (bean threads),
   very thin spaghetti or fine egg noodles
1 small whole boned skinned chicken breast
   (about 5 ounces), halved, trimmed of fat and
   cut into ½-inch pieces (about ⅔ cup)
½ teaspoon salt, divided
¼ teaspoon hot pepper sauce
Minced parsley or cilantro (optional)

Pierce deeply at least 1 eye of coconut and drain liquid into measuring cup; reserve (there should be about ⅓ to ½ cup). Crack coconut open and extract meat; cut into small pieces (you should have at least 2 ⅓ cups). Put pieces in food processor or blender with the milk. Blend about 1 to 2 minutes or until coconut is finely chopped. Transfer mixture to several thicknesses of cheesecloth set into bowl. Bring edges of cheesecloth up over coconut mixture to form a bag, completely enclosing coconut. Holding bag closed with one hand, squeeze firmly with other hand to extract ½ cup liquid (coconut cream);

reserve liquid. Return ground coconut to food processor or blender and add the water. Blend 1 to 2 minutes or until very well blended. Strain again in several thicknesses of cheesecloth, squeezing out 2 cups of liquid (coconut milk); reserve. Discard ground coconut. Melt butter in heavy large saucepan. Add onion and celery and cook over medium to medium-high heat about 10 minutes or until onion is tender, stirring occasionally. Stir in reserved coconut juice (⅓ to ½ cup), 2 cups coconut milk and the chicken broth. Bring to the boiling point, add the noodles and cook gently about 5 minutes or until noodles are al dente, stirring once or twice. (If using cellophane noodles or very thin spaghetti, cut into 3- to 4-inch lengths with kitchen shears.) Toss chicken pieces with ¼ teaspoon salt and add to noodle mixture. Stir in reserved ½ cup coconut cream, the hot pepper sauce and the remaining ¼ teaspoon salt. Simmer about 5 to 10 minutes or just until chicken is tender and soup is very hot. If desired, garnish each serving with a little minced parsley or cilantro. Serve hot or thoroughly chilled.

*Look for a coconut that is heavy for its size and sounds full of liquid when shaken. Avoid a coconut with moldy or wet eyes (the three rings at one end). To prepare coconut for recipe, use screwdriver, ice pick, barbecue skewer or other sharp pointed utensil to deeply pierce ¼-inch diameter hole in 1 or more eyes of coconut. Drain liquid from coconut into measuring cup; reserve. Tap coconut all over with hammer, then hit very hard at widest part; break open. With knife, pry out meat and pare off dark skin.

NONA'S CURRIED SOUP WITH BEAN THREADS

4 TO 6 SERVINGS

3 tablespoons oil, preferably peanut
2 large onions, halved and very thinly sliced (2 cups)
2 tablespoons curry powder
1 tablespoon ground coriander
6 cups chicken broth
2 ounces cellophane noodles (bean threads), very thin spaghetti or fine egg noodles
Minced parsley or cilantro

Heat the oil in large heavy saucepan. Add the onions and cook over medium to medium-high heat, stirring occasionally, until onions are very tender but not browned, about 10 minutes. Add curry powder and coriander and cook, over low heat, stirring constantly, 2 to 3 minutes. Add chicken broth. Bring to the boiling point. Add noodles and boil gently about 5 minutes or until noodles are tender, stirring once or twice. With kitchen shears cut noodles into 3- to 4-inch lengths. Simmer uncovered 5 more minutes or until flavors are blended. If desired, garnish each serving with parsley or cilantro.

——— • • • ———

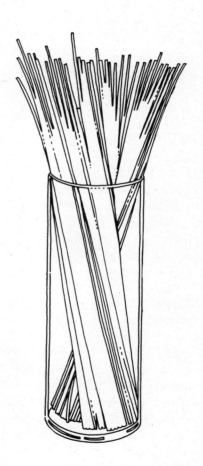

OYSTER STEW

I served oyster stew with elbow macaroni when I had no pilot crackers in the house. It was a success, especially since I added (again not traditional) a little Worcestershire and a few drops of hot pepper sauce to the stew. Any small short pasta will do for this dish. It is easy to make, but you must remember never to boil the stew; just simmer it until very hot.

4 SERVINGS

3 cups milk
1 cup heavy cream
2 cups (1 pint) shucked oysters (if large, cut
    into halves) and their liquor
1 teaspoon Worcestershire sauce
4 drops hot pepper sauce
¼ cup (½ stick) butter, cut into pieces and at
    room temperature
4 to 6 ounces elbow macaroni, freshly cooked
    al dente and drained
Freshly ground pepper

Combine milk and cream in a heavy saucepan or double boiler top. Heat but do not scald nor boil; this is best done over simmering water. Turn the oysters and their liquid into a small saucepan. Place over very low heat until the oysters are heated and begin to curl at the edges; do not boil. Remove from heat; with a slotted spoon, transfer the oysters to a bowl and reserve. Add the oyster liquor to the milk mix-ture and again heat but do not boil. Add the Worcestershire and pepper sauce and simmer gently for 2 to 3 minutes; do not boil. Add the oysters and heat through. Add the butter and stir over very low heat just until the butter has melted. Divide pasta between 4 heated soup bowls and pour oyster stew over it. Sprinkle with pepper and serve at once.

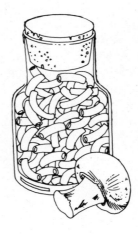

PORK AND CARDAMON STEW FOR THIN SPAGHETTI

This dish calls for a thin but sturdy pasta like thin spaghetti or linguine.

6 SERVINGS

¼ cup butter or vegetable oil
2 pounds boneless lean pork, cut into 1½-inch cubes
2 large onions, minced (about 2 cups)
2 garlic cloves, minced
2 tablespoons minced fresh ginger or to taste
2 tablespoons flour
1 cup chicken or beef bouillon
5 teaspoons ground cardamon
4 ounces snow peas, trimmed, cut into squares and blanched*
2 medium-size sweet red peppers, seeded and cut into thin strips
1 pound thin spaghetti, freshly cooked al dente and drained
Salt
Freshly ground pepper

Heat the butter or oil in a heavy large frying pan. Add the pork and cook over high heat, stirring constantly, until browned on all sides. Transfer the meat to a flameproof casserole, preferably one that can go to the table. In the same frying pan, cook the onions, garlic and ginger for 2 to 3 minutes, adding a little more butter or oil if necessary. Stir in the flour and cook for another 2 minutes. Add the bouillon and 3 teaspoons of the cardamon and bring to the boiling point. Pour sauce over pork and cover the casserole. Place over low heat and simmer for 1 hour or until the pork is fork tender and the sauce has thickened; stir frequently and add a little more bouillon or hot water if sauce is too thick. Just before serving, add the snow peas, red peppers and the remaining 2 teaspoons of cardamon;* heat through thoroughly. Add spaghetti to casserole and toss. Season with salt and pepper. Alternatively, turn spaghetti into a heated deep serving dish and top with the stew.

*To blanch snow peas, cover with boiling water and let stand for 3 minutes. Drain well.

*Ground cardamon loses flavor in cooking; that's why some is added to the stew just before serving.

· · ·

QUICK MADEIRA OR SHERRY STEW

This recipe is easily doubled or tripled. Grated cheese is not needed.

2 TO 3 SERVINGS

 1 tablespoon butter
 1 tablespoon vegetable oil
 1 small onion, minced
12 ounces top or bottom round or any tender beef, cut into 1 × 3-inch strips
 1 medium tomato, peeled and diced or ½ cup tomato sauce
⅓ cup dry Madeira, Sherry or Marsala
¼ teaspoon dried marjoram or thyme
Salt
Freshly ground pepper
 6 to 8 ounces long or short small pasta, freshly cooked al dente and drained

Heat the butter and oil in a large deep frying pan over medium-high heat. Add the onion and cook, stirring constantly, for 3 to 4 minutes or until soft and golden. Add the meat and cook over medium heat, stirring constantly with a fork until brown on all sides. Reduce heat to low, add all the other ingredients except the pasta and simmer for about 10 minutes. Turn pasta into a heated serving dish and pour stew over it. Toss at the table.

SIMPLE ORIENTAL SOUP WITH NOODLES

4 TO 6 SERVINGS

 2 ounces transparent cellophane noodles (bean threads)
10 to 12 cups water or chicken bouillon or half water, half bouillon
 6 green onions, cut into 3-inch pieces
 8 ounces boneless lean pork, cut into ½ × 1½-inch strips
 8 ounces snow peas, halved
 4 ounces mushrooms, sliced or quartered
 1 to 2 tablespoons sesame oil (optional)
 1 tablespoon grated lemon peel
 2 teaspoons soy sauce or to taste
Freshly ground pepper

Place noodles in a deep bowl and cover with boiling water. Let stand for 30 minutes or until thoroughly softened. Cut noodles in half with kitchen shears so they will be easier to manage when eating. Combine the 10 to 12 cups water, green onions, and pork in a kettle. Bring to boiling point, cover and simmer over low heat for 20 minutes. Add snow peas and mushrooms and simmer for 10 more minutes. Stir in sesame oil, lemon peel, soy sauce, and pepper and cook for 2 to 3 more minutes. Drain noodles and add to soup. Serve immediately.

Sturdy Country Vegetable Stew

Use tiny elbows, tiny rings, orzo or other soup pastina about the size of a grain of rice or two. Bread, cheese and a fruit dessert complete the meal.

6 SERVINGS

1 cup dried white navy beans, washed
3½ to 4 cups chicken or beef bouillon
2 medium potatoes, peeled and cut into ½-inch pieces
2 large carrots, sliced
2 medium artichokes, thinly sliced (optional)*
2 medium to large zucchini, thinly sliced
2 leeks (white and green parts), sliced or 1 bunch green onions, (white and green parts), sliced
1 turnip, cut into ½-inch pieces
1 cup soup pastina
2 pounds fresh peas, shelled or one 10-ounce package frozen peas (about 2 cups)
Salt
Freshly ground pepper
¾ teaspoon ground sage
½ cup (1 stick) butter, melted
Freshly grated Parmesan cheese

Pour boiling water to cover over the beans and let stand for 1 hour (or soak beans in water overnight) and drain. Place beans in a large kettle and add cold water to cover. Cook over medium heat for 30 minutes or until almost but not completely tender. Add 3 cups of bouillon and bring to the boiling point. Add potatoes, carrots, artichokes, zucchini, leeks and turnip and cook over high heat for about 4 minutes. Add another ½ cup bouillon and pastina. Cover and cook over medium heat, stirring frequently, until the pastina is almost tender. Add peas and season with salt and pepper. If mixture is too thick, add bouillon 2 tablespoons at a time until desired consistency. Stir sage into the melted butter and stir into stew. Serve hot or warm with plenty of grated Parmesan.

*Strip off tough outer leaves of artichokes, trim spiky tops from remaining leaves and cut off all but ¼ inch of stem. Cut artichokes into quarters; remove chokes and slice. To prevent darkening, keep pieces submerged in water with a little vinegar or lemon juice until they are needed.

THICK PASTA AND BEAN SOUP

Pasta e Fazul, as this is called in southern Italy, is a tasty and satisfying but humble soup. To give it true flavor, it should be made with lard rather than olive oil, and preferably with pancetta, salt pork, or bacon. Like all popular Italian soups, it can be made as thin or as thick as desired by adjusting the liquid.

6 SERVINGS

8 ounces dried pinto, navy, or other small
  beans, washed
1 quart water
6 cups hot beef bouillon or water
1 cup tomato sauce
2 tablespoons lard or olive oil
½ cup minced pancetta, salt pork or bacon
1 medium onion, minced
1 celery rib, minced
1 garlic clove, minced
1 tablespoon flour
Salt
½ teaspoon crushed dried hot pepper flakes or
  freshly ground pepper
½ teaspoon oregano
6 to 8 ounces ditalini or other small pasta
½ cup chopped parsley
Freshly grated Parmesan cheese

Pour boiling water to cover over beans and let stand for 1 hour (or soak beans in water overnight) and drain. Cook beans in the 1 quart water until they taste half tender. Add bouillon and tomato sauce and continue to cook. Meanwhile, heat the lard in a skillet. Add the pancetta, onion, celery and garlic and cook over medium heat, stirring constantly, for 3 to 5 minutes; do not brown. Stir in the flour and about 1 cup of the liquid in which the beans are cooking and stir until smooth. Add to the beans. Season with salt (cautiously, since bouillon and pancetta will be salty), pepper and oregano. Cover and simmer over low heat until the beans are almost tender. Add the ditalini and cook, stirring frequently, until tender. Sprinkle with parsley and serve hot or warm with grated Parmesan.

＿＿＿　• • •　＿＿＿

Salads

Danish Macaroni Salad

Easy Chicken Salad Orientale

Macaroni-Egg Salad

Noodle Salami Salad

Pasta Salad with Sesame Seed

Pasta Salad with Smoked Chicken or
Turkey

Shiny Noodle Salad with Shrimp

Spicy Peanut Noodle Salad

Summer Orzo Salad

PASTA SALADS

Pasta salads have become fashionable summer fare. Italians are surprised at this because, except for a few southern specialties, pasta is traditionally eaten hot in Italy. In truth it must be said that today some restaurants in Italy, catering to American tourists, are beginning to feature these summer salads. Let us hope that these pasta dishes do not include the often horrible combinations of their American counterparts, sold all too often in so-called "gourmet" shops.

Here are a few basic considerations for the construction of an honest pasta salad.

1) The pasta that is suitable for salads is the "short" pasta such as elbows, tubes, spirals, etc., which will catch the sauce. Tortellini, ravioli and other stuffed pastas are totally unacceptable because their stuffing congeals to an unpleasant flavor and consistency when chilled. Use dry commercial pasta for salads, since fresh pasta is too delicate for the purpose and becomes mushy. However, Oriental pasta, though long like cellophane noodles, lends itself to salads.

How to cook pasta for salads

To keep the pasta from becoming sticky when cold, add one to two tablespoons oil to the cooking water (some cooks do this for hot pasta as well, though it is not strictly necessary). The water for pasta salads should be more heavily salted; please remember that most of the salt is washed off when the cooked pasta for salad is rinsed off under cold running water.

Be sure to keep the pasta strictly al dente when making a pasta salad. Over-cooked pasta will not stand up to dressing and chilling. If you want to, chill the pasta before dressing it. Serve it chilled, or preferably at room temperature, which prevents clamminess.

2) Since pasta salads should be fresh and light, fresh vegetables, seafood and light meats like chicken are the most appropriate combinations. Any cooked vegetable salads are good mixed with cold pasta, as is even a simple vinaigrette laced with herbs. And you don't need grated cheese on these dishes. If you use raw vegetables, avoid (or cut into very small pieces) those that may be too hard to chew.

3) Pasta salad dressings should be flavorful and as piquant as you like them. Wine vinegars, capers, anchovies and fresh herbs add to this piquancy. The dressing should be freshly made.

——— · · · ———

Danish Macaroni Salad

A mild dish that goes well with a flavorful baked ham, as served in Denmark. Serve slightly, not thoroughly, chilled.

4 TO 6 SERVINGS

8 ounces elbow or small shell macaroni
2 cups heavy cream
2 teaspoons sugar
Salt
Freshly ground white pepper
2 to 3 tablespoons grated fresh or drained
    bottled horseradish
2 teaspoons white vinegar or to taste
2 tablespoons minced fresh dill, chives or
    parsley or to taste

Cook the pasta in plenty of rapidly boiling salted water until al dente. Drain and rinse under cold running water. Drain again; chill for 30 minutes. Whip the cream until stiff. Season with sugar, salt, and pepper. Stir in the horseradish, vinegar, and half of the dill. Add cooked pasta and mix well. Turn into a serving dish and sprinkle with the remaining dillweed.

· · ·

EASY CHICKEN SALAD ORIENTALE

Like all pasta salads, this tastes better at room temperature than chilled.

2 TO 4 SERVINGS

4 ounces Chinese noodles, thin spaghetti or fettucine
2 cups diced cooked chicken
2 tablespoons peanut or vegetable oil
2 tablespoons sesame oil
1 teaspoon chili oil (optional)
2 tablespoons white or red wine vinegar
½ to 1 teaspoon ground ginger or 1 tablespoon fresh minced ginger (optional)
1 cup fresh bean sprouts, rinsed in cold water and drained
1 cucumber, cut into julienne strips
Salt
Freshly ground black pepper
3 green onions, white and green parts, thinly sliced
Salad greens

Cook the noodles in plenty of rapidly boiling salted water until just al dente. Drain and rinse under cold running water; drain well. Place chicken in a bowl and add the oils, vinegar, and ginger. Toss to mix thoroughly. If possible, let stand at room temperature for 15 minutes, or refrigerate covered for 1 hour. Line the bottom of a serving dish with the noodles. Top with the bean sprouts, chicken and cucumber. Season lightly with salt, if wanted, and pepper. Sprinkle with the green onions. Arrange salad leaves around the edges of the serving dish. Toss salad at the table.

———   • • •   ———

MACARONI-EGG SALAD

Serve with washed and dried salad greens; garnish with tomatoes if desired.

4 TO 6 SERVINGS

1 cup mayonnaise or ½ cup mayonnaise and ½ cup sour cream or yogurt
2 tablespoons minced onion or green onion
1 garlic clove, minced (optional)
1 teaspoon Dijon mustard or to taste
8 ounces elbow, spiral or small shell macaroni or other small open-end pasta, freshly cooked al dente and drained
6 hard cooked eggs, chopped
1 cup chopped Swiss or Cheddar cheese
1 cup thinly sliced celery
Salt
Freshly ground pepper
Salad greens
2 tablespoons minced parsley or chives

In a large non-metal bowl, combine mayonnaise, onion, garlic clove and mustard and mix well. Add macaroni, eggs, cheese and celery and mix well. Season with salt and pepper. Cover with plastic wrap and refrigerate until used. At serving time, line a salad bowl with salad greens and mound salad on greens. Sprinkle with parsley and serve immediately.

Note: Leftovers can be refrigerated for a day, but remove salad greens first.

— · · · —

NOODLE SALAMI SALAD
8 TO 10 SERVINGS

8 ounces thin spaghetti or thin egg noodles
4 ounces thinly sliced salami, cut into ¼-inch strips, then strips halved crosswise
1 medium cucumber, halved lengthwise and very thinly sliced (1 cup)
1 large red onion, halved and very thinly sliced (1 cup)
1 cup peeled diced tomato (2 medium)
1½ quarts bite-size pieces crisp romaine lettuce (1 medium head)

Lime Soy Dressing (see recipe)
Garnish: thin cucumber slices, red onion slices, or tomato wedges

Cook spaghetti in rapidly boiling salted water for 8 to 10 minutes or until al dente. Drain and rinse under cold running water; drain well. Cut with kitchen shears into 3- to 4-inch lengths. In a large bowl toss spaghetti, salami, cucumber, onion, tomato and romaine. Pour dressing and toss well. Garnish with cucumber, red onion or tomato. Serve at room temperature.

Salad can be made ahead and chilled, then brought to room temperature. Toss in romaine and salt, if desired, just before serving.

LIME SOY DRESSING
Makes about 1⅛ cups

½ cup fresh lime juice
⅓ cup sesame or peanut oil
⅓ cup soy sauce
3 tablespoons sugar
1 large garlic clove, minced

Blend all ingredients in small bowl.

— · · · —

PASTA SALAD WITH SESAME SEED

6 SERVINGS

8 ounces capellini (very thin spaghetti) or fresh Chinese egg noodles
1 cup diagonally sliced green onions with part tops (about 10 medium)
2 cups julienne-cut cucumbers (about 1 × ⅛ or 1 × ¼ inch)—about 2 medium cucumbers
4 cups watercress leaves
¼ cup sesame seed, lightly toasted
Soy Sauce Dressing (see recipe)
Garnish: Sliced green onion, julienne-cut cucumber, watercress sprigs

Cook pasta in rapidly boiling salted water until al dente, about 3 to 5 minutes, stirring once or twice. Drain and rinse under cold running water; drain well. Cut with kitchen shears into 3- to 4-inch lengths. In a large bowl toss together drained pasta, green onions, cucumbers, watercress and sesame seed. Pour on dressing and toss well. Garnish with sliced green onion, cucumber strips and watercress sprigs. Serve at room temperature.

Salad can be made ahead and chilled, then brought to room temperature. Toss in watercress just before serving.

SOY SAUCE DRESSING
Makes about 1⅛ cups

⅓ cup sesame or peanut oil
⅓ cup soy sauce
3 tablespoons fresh lemon juice
3 tablespoons dry Sherry
2 tablespoons sugar
1 tablespoon minced fresh ginger
Chili oil or hot pepper sauce to taste

Blend all ingredients in small bowl.

PASTA SALAD WITH SMOKED CHICKEN OR TURKEY

Use any very small pasta such as orzo, small elbows, or tubettini. Assemble the salad at serving time and remember that avocados, even when sprinkled with lemon juice, darken with prolonged standing.

3 to 4 cups freshly cooked small pasta, drained, rinsed under cold running water and drained well
1 pound smoked chicken or turkey, cut into bite-size pieces (about 4 cups)
1 cup peeled, seeded and diced tomatoes
1 large avocado, pitted, peeled, cut into ½-inch pieces and sprinkled with 1 tablespoon fresh lemon juice
¾ cup diced red onion
¾ cup olive oil
¼ cup red wine vinegar

3 tablespoons minced parsley
½ teaspoon Dijon mustard
Salt
Freshly ground pepper

Combine the pasta, turkey, tomatoes, avocado and onion in a large serving dish or salad bowl and toss lightly and quickly with two forks. Combine the oil, vinegar, parsley, mustard, very little salt (meat and mustard are salty), and pepper and mix well. Pour over the salad and toss just to blend. Serve immediately.

SHINY NOODLE SALAD WITH SHRIMP
6 SERVINGS

5 ounces cellophane noodles (bean threads) or 8 ounces spaghetti
8 ounces shrimp
2 cups water
½ teaspoon salt
2 medium cucumbers, cut lengthwise in eighths, then sliced diagonally crosswise (2 cups)
1 large red onion, minced (1 cup)
1 cup peeled diced tomato (2 medium)
Hot Sweet Lime Dressing (see recipe)
Salt (optional)
Garnish: Thinly sliced red onion or cucumber, or tomato or lime wedges

Cook pasta in rapidly boiling salted water until tender, about 5 minutes for cellophane noodles and 9 minutes for spaghetti, stirring once or twice. Drain and rinse under cold running water; drain well. Cut with kitchen shears into 3- to 4-inch lengths. In saucepan bring shrimp, 2 cups water and salt to boiling point and cook just until shrimp is tender, 1 to 2 minutes. Drain; rinse under cold water. Remove shells. Cut shrimps in half lengthwise; devein. Rinse once more under cold water and pat dry. Cut shrimp into small pieces (you should have about 1 cup). In large bowl toss noodles, shrimp, cucumbers, red onion, and tomato until combined. Pour on dressing and toss well. Season with salt if desired. Garnish with red onion or cucumber slices and/or tomato or lime wedges. Serve at room temperature, spooning some of the dressing from bottom of serving bowl onto each serving.

HOT SWEET LIME DRESSING
Makes generous ¾ cup

½ cup fresh lime juice
¼ cup sugar
2 tablespoons sesame oil
2 tablespoons soy sauce
1 large garlic clove, minced
¾ teaspoon crushed dried hot pepper flakes

Blend all ingredients in small bowl.

—————— · · · ——————

SPICY PEANUT NOODLE SALAD

8 TO 10 SERVINGS

1½ cups fresh bean sprouts or one 14-ounce can
1 cup chicken bouillon
1 whole boned skinned chicken breast (about 6 ounces), halved and trimmed of fat
8 ounces thin linguine or Japanese water noodles (udon)
1 cup diagonally sliced green onions with part tops (about 10 medium)
1 cup shredded radishes (8 to 10 large)
½ cup salted peanuts, chopped
¼ teaspoon salt
Spicy Peanut Butter Dressing (see recipe)
Garnish: Sliced green onions, shredded radishes, or chopped peanuts

Wash fresh bean sprouts thoroughly and drain well; if using canned bean sprouts, drain and rinse well under cold water. Chill sprouts in ice water for 30 minutes to crisp. Drain well; set aside. In small saucepan bring chicken bouillon to boiling point. Add chicken and simmer uncovered 5 to 8 minutes or just until chicken is tender. Drain, reserving bouillon for another use. Cool the chicken. When cool enough to handle, cut the chicken into 1 × ¼-inch julienne strips using kitchen shears (you will have about 1 cup). Cook linguine in rapidly boiling salted water until al dente, about 8 minutes, stirring once or twice. Drain and rinse under cold running water; drain well. Cut with kitchen shears into 3- to 4-inch lengths. In a large bowl combine the crisped bean sprouts, chicken, linguine, green onions, radishes, peanuts and salt. Pour on dressing and toss well. Garnish with sliced green onions, shredded radishes or chopped peanuts if desired. Serve at room temperature.

Salad can be made ahead and chilled, then brought to room temperature. Toss in bean sprouts and peanuts just before serving.

SPICY PEANUT BUTTER DRESSING
Makes about 1 cup

¼ cup creamy peanut butter
¼ cup soy sauce
¼ cup peanut or sesame oil
¼ cup water
3 tablespoons fresh lemon juice
1 tablespoon firmly packed brown sugar
1 large garlic clove, minced
½ teaspoon cayenne pepper or to taste

Whisk together all ingredients in small bowl.

_____ • • • _____

SUMMER ORZO SALAD

This is a Moroccan-inspired summer salad which is different, but not so different as to scare conservative eaters. It is a "more-or-less" dish that can be adjusted to taste, especially in the seasonings. Since orzo is not as well known as some other pastas, I specify water and salt amounts for its cooking. 1 level cup raw orzo yields about 3 cups cooked.

10 TO 12 SERVINGS

4 quarts water
2 teaspoons salt
2 cups orzo
1 to 2 medium zucchini (about 12 ounces), coarsely chopped or diced (about 3 cups)
1 can (16 ounces) garbanzo beans, rinsed under cold running water and drained well (about 2 cups)
4 medium carrots, coarsely chopped or diced (about 1¾ cups)
1 to 2 large tomatoes, peeled and diced (about 1¼ cups)
1 large onion, minced (about 1 cup)
½ cup golden raisins, plumped in warm water and drained
½ cup chopped pitted dates
6 tablespoons olive oil
¼ cup fresh lemon juice
¼ teaspoon ground ginger
¼ teaspoon turmeric
¼ teaspoon cinnamon
Salt
Freshly ground pepper
½ cup toasted slivered almonds
Garnish: Toasted slivered almonds

Bring water to boil in a large kettle. Add the salt and slowly sprinkle in the orzo. Return to rapid boil and cook, stirring occasionally, for about 10 minutes or until the orzo is tender but not mushy; do not overcook. Drain in a large fine-meshed strainer or colander; rinse under cold running water and drain thoroughly. In a large salad or serving bowl combine the orzo, zucchini, garbanzo beans, carrots, tomatoes, onion, raisins and dates. In a small bowl, whisk together the oil, lemon juice, ginger, turmeric, cinnamon, about 1½ teaspoons salt and pepper. Blend thoroughly. Pour over orzo mixture and toss gently with 2 forks until well mixed. Sprinkle with the almonds. Serve at room temperature, with more toasted slivered almonds on the side. If the salad has been chilled, allow it to return to room temperature before serving for the best flavor. Do not chill it or let it stand for too long or the vegetables will lose their crispness.

——— • • • ———

Pasta–Plain and with Cheese

Alsatian Noodles

Best Macaroni and Cheese

Bobby's Noodle Pudding

Easy Spinach Pasta with Cream, Pine Nuts, and Basil

Greened Thin Pasta

Hungarian Noodles

Pasta Pancake

Pasta with Vodka, Cream, and Tomato Sauce

Pasta Piccante

Rich Macaroni and Cheese

Simple Baked Fettucine or Noodles

Spaghetti Aglio e Olio

Spaghetti Polonaise

Thin Egg Noodles with Ricotta

White and/or Green Noodles with Four Cheeses

ALSATIAN NOODLES

The texture contrast between soft and crisp fried noodles is interesting. This is best as a side dish.

4 SERVINGS

8 ounces narrow egg noodles
3 tablespoons butter
⅔ cup grated Swiss cheese
Salt
Freshly ground pepper
2 tablespoons vegetable oil

Cook the noodles in rapidly boiling salted water until al dente. Drain well. Divide the noodles in half; reserve one portion. Melt the butter in a frying pan. Add half the noodles, stir in the cheese, salt and pepper, and cook over low heat, stirring constantly, for 3 to 5 minutes. Remove pan from heat and keep warm. Heat the oil in another frying pan. Add the remaining noodles and cook over medium heat, stirring constantly with a fork until the noodles are golden and crisp but not hard. Turn the cheesed noodles into a heated serving dish and sprinkle with the fried noodles. Toss at the table and serve immediately.

• • •

BEST MACARONI AND CHEESE

A far cry from the ordinary, macaroni-and-white-cheese-sauce M and C.

4 TO 6 SERVINGS

8 ounces elbow macaroni
3 tablespoons butter
¼ cup minced onion or shallots
3 tablespoons flour
Salt
Freshly ground pepper
Cayenne pepper to taste
1 cup light cream or half-and-half
½ cup dry white wine or ⅓ cup dry vermouth
8 ounces grated sharp Cheddar cheese

Cook macaroni in plenty of rapidly boiling salted water until not quite al dente (macaroni will be cooked again and must not be mushy). Drain, turn into a bowl, and reserve. Melt butter in a medium saucepan. Add onion and cook over low heat, stirring constantly, until onion is soft but not colored. Stir in the flour, salt, pepper and cayenne and cook for 2 more minutes. Combine the cream and wine, add to onion mixture and cook, stirring constantly, until the sauce is thick and smooth. Stir in the cheese and cook, stirring constantly, until melted. Pour cheese sauce over macaroni and toss to mix thoroughly. Turn into a generously buttered 1½-quart baking dish. Bake in a preheated 350°F oven for about 20 minutes or until top is golden brown. Serve immediately.

——— • • • ———

BOBBY'S NOODLE PUDDING

A very rich side dish—worth eating.

4 TO 6 SERVINGS

8 ounces medium noodles
6 tablespoons (¾ stick) butter
Salt
Freshly ground pepper
2 cups creamed cottage cheese, at room
  temperature
2 cups sour cream, at room temperature

Cook the noodles in plenty of rapidly boiling salted water until almost but not quite al dente. Drain and turn into a generously buttered 1½-quart baking dish. Toss with 3 to 4 tablespoons of the butter, salt and plenty of pepper. Stir in cottage cheese and sour cream and mix well. Dot with the remaining butter. Bake in a preheated 350°F oven for about 20 minutes or until top is golden brown. Serve immediately.

EASY SPINACH PASTA WITH CREAM, PINE NUTS AND BASIL

It is not absolutely necessary that you use spinach noodles, but they look pretty and taste good in this dish.

4 SERVINGS

8 to 12 ounces spinach ziti (or other green
  pasta), freshly cooked al dente and drained
⅔ to 1 cup butter, at room temperature and
  cut into small pieces
½ cup heavy cream, heated
¼ cup minced fresh basil leaves or to taste
Salt
Freshly ground pepper
⅔ cup pine nuts
1 cup freshly grated Parmesan cheese

Turn the pasta into a deep heated serving dish. Add the butter, cream, and basil and toss quickly with two forks. Season with salt (cautiously; cheese will be salty) and pepper. Add pine nuts and cheese, toss again and serve immediately.

——— • • • ———

Greened Thin Pasta

This creamy green sauce must go over very thin spaghetti or fettucine; but, for reasons I cannot fathom, it is not right for the thinnest pasta, angels' hair. You may also add a little chopped fresh basil, thyme, sage or other herb to the sauce, but do not use dried herbs if you can help it. I think it is a good idea, though not entirely necessary, to blanch the parsley first by pouring boiling water over it and letting it stand for 2 to 3 minutes before draining it. This removes the raw taste of the herb.

ABOUT 2¾ CUPS SAUCE;
4 SERVINGS

12 to 16 ounces thin pasta
1½ cups (3 sticks) butter, at room temperature and cut into small pieces
2 garlic cloves, minced
2 cups freshly grated Parmesan cheese
2 cups tightly packed minced Italian or curly parsley
Salt
Freshly ground pepper

Cook the pasta in plenty of rapidly boiling salted water. Drain and return to pot immediately. Add butter, garlic, cheese and parsley, cover pot and shake vigorously to mix. Adjust seasoning with salt and add pepper. Cover the pot and toss again. Turn into a very hot deep serving dish or divide between four heated plates or bowls and serve immediately.

Hungarian Noodles

Serve as a side dish instead of potatoes or rice.

___4 SERVINGS___

8 ounces medium egg noodles
¼ cup (½ stick) butter
1 small onion, minced
¼ cup fine dry breadcrumbs
1 to 1½ tablespoons poppyseed or caraway
   seed
Salt
Freshly ground pepper

Cook noodles in plenty of boiling water until softened but still very al dente. Drain and keep warm. While noodles are cooking, melt the butter in a deep 10- to 12-inch frying pan. Add onion and cook until soft but not browned. Add the breadcrumbs, poppyseed and noodles and toss lightly with a fork to mix. Season with salt and pepper. Cook over medium heat, stirring constantly, for about 3 to 4 minutes, or until heated through. Turn into a heated serving dish and serve immediately.

Pasta Pancake

An extremely practical and tasty dish. Use fresh, leftover plain, or leftover sauced pasta—any long or short pasta that is already cooked and that you think would lend itself to being fried with eggs and milk. It goes well with cold cuts and a salad.

___4 SERVINGS___

12 ounces noodles or other pasta, cooked and
    drained
 2 to 3 eggs
⅓ cup milk
⅓ cup freshly grated cheese (optional)
Salt
Freshly ground pepper
¼ cup (½ stick) butter or margarine

Place noodles in a large bowl. Beat together eggs, milk, cheese, salt and pepper, pour over noodles and toss to mix thoroughly. Melt the butter in a large deep frying pan. Add the noodle mixture and stir with a fork to spread evenly over the frying pan. Cook over low heat until eggs are set and bottom of the pancake is crusty. If you want a golden brown crust on the other side, put a serving plate over the frying pan and flip the pancake onto it; flip it back into the frying pan with the browned side on top. Cook over low heat until browned on the underside. Serve pancake hot or warm.

PASTA WITH VODKA, CREAM AND TOMATO SAUCE

From Italy's new and very sophisticated restaurants. It is essential to use a flavorful vodka, preferably Polish or Russian, because the flavor remains as the alcohol cooks away. I use green penne for this dish, but the sauce is also good on egg noodles. It is quite powerful and the pasta should not be too delicate.

ABOUT 3½ CUPS SAUCE;
5 TO 6 SERVINGS

1 pound green penne or ziti
½ cup (1 stick) butter
¾ cup good quality vodka
½ teaspoon dried hot pepper flakes* or to taste**
¼ teaspoon Worcestershire sauce
1 cup *thick* tomato sauce
1 cup heavy cream
Salt
Freshly ground pepper
1½ cups freshly grated Parmesan cheese
Additional freshly grated Parmesan cheese

Cook the pasta in plenty of boiling salted water until just al dente. Drain well. While pasta is cooking, make the sauce. Melt the butter in a flameproof casserole that is large enough to hold all the pasta and can go to the table. Add vodka, pepper flakes, and Worcestershire, mix well and simmer over low to medium heat for about 5 minutes. Blend in tomato sauce and cream and bring to the boiling point. Simmer for about 5 minutes or until the sauce has thickened slightly. Season with a little salt (be careful; cheese will be salty) and pepper. Add the hot drained pasta to the sauce and toss well. Reduce heat to very low and stir in cheese. Serve immediately with additional Parmesan.

*Dried red hot pepper flakes can be bought or made at home. Use the dried red hot peppers sold in Mediterranean and Oriental groceries. Split them open with fingers and remove all the seeds and membranes, which are the hottest parts. Do this under running cold water. Then crumble the peppers and measure ½ teaspoon crumbled pepper. Put it on a saucer and add about 2 tablespoons water to soften it before cooking. Let stand for 10 to 15 minutes. Then proceed as in recipe, using both flakes and water in which they were soaked. IMPORTANT. While working with peppers, do not touch your face nor eyes. Wash your hands thoroughly with hot water and soap before touching yourself or any other food, since hot peppers can burn you.

**The dish must be peppery, but since people vary in their tolerance to hot foods, it is better to use less hot pepper than too much. I put a bottle of hot pepper sauce on the dining table for those who want to hot up their dish.

Pasta Piccante
Piquant Pasta

This is the reconstruction of a dish made for me by an elegant Italian friend many years ago in Rome. You can spice it up or down as you wish. I find it to be more an appetizer pasta than a main dish. My friend made it with spaghetti, but I prefer thin to medium egg noodles.

ABOUT 1½ CUPS SAUCE;
3 TO 4 SERVINGS

6 to 8 ounces egg noodles or spaghetti
½ cup (1 stick) butter
½ teaspoon dried hot pepper flakes or to taste
¼ teaspoon Worcestershire sauce
½ cup Cognac or brandy
¾ cup heavy cream (or more)
Salt
Freshly ground pepper
1 cup freshly grated Parmesan cheese
Additional freshly grated Parmesan cheese

Cook the noodles in plenty of boiling salted water until just al dente; drain. While water is boiling and pasta is cooking, prepare the sauce. Melt the butter in a flameproof casserole that is large enough to hold all the pasta and can go to the table. Add pepper flakes, Worcestershire sauce and half of the Cognac and mix well. Simmer over low heat for about 5 minutes. Add the cream and bring to boil. Simmer for about 3 to 4 minutes or until the cream has thickened a little and the sauce is heated through. Stir in the remaining Cognac, a little salt (be careful; cheese will be salty) and pepper. Add the hot drained pasta to the sauce and toss well. Reduce heat to very low and stir in cheese. Serve immediately with additional Parmesan.

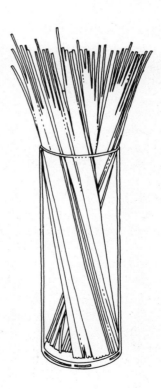

RICH MACARONI AND CHEESE

4 SERVINGS

8 ounces elbow macaroni, small ziti, shells or
  any small pasta with holes to absorb sauce
2 cups heavy cream
1 tablespoon grated onion or shallot
¾ to 1 teaspoon ground saffron or crumbled
  saffron threads
4 ounces grated or shredded Swiss cheese
Salt
Freshly ground pepper
1 medium zucchini, trimmed and cut into ¼
  inch slices
2 tablespoons minced chives or parsley

Cook macaroni in plenty of boiling salted water
until barely al dente. Drain and return to cooking pot; cover pot and keep warm. While macaroni is cooking, combine cream, grated onion
and saffron in a wide shallow saucepan and
bring slowly to boil. Cook over low heat until
reduced to about 1½ cups (watch cream carefully to prevent boiling over). Stir in the cheese
and cook over low heat, stirring constantly, until
cheese is melted. Pour mixture over cooked
macaroni. Adjust seasoning with salt and pepper. Mix well and place over lowest possible
heat just to heat through, stirring constantly.
Line heated serving dish with zucchini slices.
Pile macaroni on top; the heat of the macaroni
will cook the zucchini al dente. Sprinkle with
minced chives or parsley and serve immediately.

SIMPLE BAKED FETTUCINE OR NOODLES

An easy side dish, and nicer with green fettucine or noodles.

4 TO 6 SERVINGS

1 pound spinach noodles
2 cups light cream or half-and-half
1½ cups freshly grated Parmesan, Romano or
    Swiss cheese
Salt
Freshly ground pepper

Cook the noodles in plenty of rapidly boiling salted water until not quite al dente (do not overcook since noodles will be baked). Drain and put in a large bowl. Toss the noodles with 1½ cups of the cream, 1 cup of cheese and salt and pepper to taste (go easy on the salt since the cheese will be salty). Turn into a generously buttered 13 × 9-inch baking dish; sprinkle with the remaining cheese. Cover the dish with foil. Bake in a preheated 350°F oven for 15 minutes or until heated through. Remove from oven, take off foil and sprinkle with the remaining cream. Return to oven for 5 more minutes. Serve immediately.

Note: You can assemble the dish ahead, cover and refrigerate it until baking time. Follow instructions up to the time the dish goes into the oven.

SPAGHETTI AGLIO E OLIO

This is a true garlic and olive oil lover's spaghetti. I use butter as well as olive oil, because I feel the butter softens the harshness of what I confess is not my favorite pasta, though all my friends love the dish. In Italy no grated cheese is served with this.

4 SERVINGS

½ cup olive oil (best possible quality)
½ cup (1 stick) butter
4 to 8 garlic cloves or to taste, minced
Salt
Freshly ground pepper
½ teaspoon oregano (optional)
½ cup minced parsley
8 ounces spaghetti, freshly cooked al dente
    and drained

Warm the olive oil and butter over low heat (mixture must be warm rather than hot or the dish will have a harsh flavor). Add the garlic and cook over low heat, stirring constantly, for 4 to 5 minutes. Stir in salt, pepper and oregano and cook for 3 more minutes, stirring. Turn spaghetti into a heated serving dish and toss with the sauce. Serve immediately.

· · ·

SPAGHETTI POLONAISE

This is best with long pasta. I think of it as a side rather than a main dish.

4 TO 6 SERVINGS

12 ounces spaghetti
 2 tablespoons (¼ stick) butter
 2 tablespoons heavy cream
Salt
Freshly ground pepper
 2 hard cooked eggs, chopped
 2 tablespoons minced parsley
 2 tablespoons freshly grated Parmesan or
   Swiss cheese
 2 tablespoons browned butter*
 1 tablespoon fresh breadcrumbs

Cook the spaghetti in plenty of rapidly boiling salted water until al dente; drain. Melt the butter in a saucepan; add the spaghetti and toss well. Add the cream, salt and pepper and toss again. Transfer to a heated serving dish and sprinkle with the hard cooked eggs, parsley and cheese. Add the breadcrumbs to the browned butter and spread over the top; if desired, brown quickly under broiler. Serve immediately, tossing again at the table.

*To brown butter, heat 3 tablespoons butter gently in a small saucepan over low heat. Cook just until nut brown in color, but no longer or the butter will burn. It is essential to keep the heat low.

THIN EGG NOODLES WITH RICOTTA

Best made with fresh homemade noodles or vermicelli.

ABOUT 3 CUPS SAUCE;
4 TO 6 SERVINGS

 1 pound narrow fresh or dried noodles
¾ cup heavy cream
 2 cups (1 pound) fresh whole or skim milk
   ricotta or one 15-ounce container
 1 tablespoon olive oil
Salt
Freshly ground white or black pepper
 2 to 3 drops hot pepper sauce or to taste
   (optional)
 1 cup freshly grated Parmesan cheese
⅔ cup chopped walnuts or to taste (optional)

Cook noodles in plenty of rapidly boiling salted water until al dente. While pasta is cooking, heat but do not boil cream in a flameproof casserole that will hold all the ingredients and can go to the table. Add the ricotta and mix with a wooden spoon or wire whisk until smooth. Stir in oil, salt and pepper to taste, hot pepper sauce and ½ cup cheese. Keep hot over a very low flame; do not boil. Drain pasta and turn it into the casserole. Add remaining Parmesan and toss well. Sprinkle with walnuts and serve immediately.

White and/or Green Noodles with Four Cheeses

A dish that has become fashionable in the everlasting quest for new ways of dressing pasta. Italian cheeses taste best, but others will do in an emergency.

ABOUT 3 CUPS SAUCE;
4 TO 6 SERVINGS

6 tablespoons (¾ stick) butter
4 ounces Fontina or Munster cheese, cut into ¼-inch cubes
4 ounces Gorgonzola or other blue-veined cheese, cut into ¼-inch cubes
4 ounces mozzarella cheese, cut into ¼-inch cubes
1 pound medium or fine green and/or white noodles
1 cup freshly grated Parmesan cheese
1 cup heavy cream
Salt
Freshly ground pepper

Melt but do not brown butter in a flameproof casserole that will hold all the ingredients and can go to the table. Add Fontina, Gorgonzola and mozzarella cheeses and cook over lowest possible heat, stirring constantly, until melted (cheese will be stringy at this point). Keep warm over lowest possible heat. Cook the noodles in plenty of rapidly boiling salted water until just al dente (cooking time will depend on whether fresh or dried pasta is used). While noodles are cooking, add Parmesan to the sauce and stir until melted. Blend in the cream. Cook over very low heat, stirring constantly, until cream is thoroughly incorporated into the cheeses; until this happens, the cheese will be stringy and separate from the cream. *Do not boil the sauce.* Adjust seasoning with salt and pepper. Drain noodles well and turn into casserole with sauce. Toss thoroughly and serve very hot.

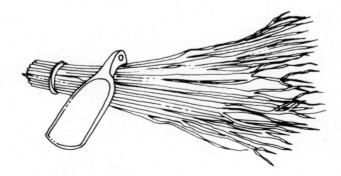

Pasta with Fish

Angels' Hair (or Very Thin Fettucine) with Sour Cream and Caviar

Egg Noodles with Smoked Salmon

Noodle- or Macaroni-Tunafish Casserole

Noodles with Mussels

Party Seafood Lasagne

Pasta with Striped Bass Sauce

Spaghetti with Swordfish in Tomato Sauce

ANGELS' HAIR (OR VERY THIN FETTUCINE) WITH SOUR CREAM AND CAVIAR

Cook—do not overcook—the pasta while making the sauce.

ABOUT 2¼ CUPS SAUCE;
4 TO 6 SERVINGS

6 tablespoons (¾ stick) butter, at room temperature
1 cup sour cream
½ cup heavy cream
Juice of 1 medium lemon
Salt
Freshly ground pepper
1 pound angels' hair or very thin fettucine, freshly cooked al dente and drained
5 ounces red or black caviar or more to taste

Melt the butter in the top of a double boiler, over hot, not boiling water. Blend in sour cream, heavy cream and lemon juice. Season with a little salt (be careful; caviar will be salty) and pepper. Keep hot over hot water but do not boil; stir frequently to prevent separation. Place cooked and drained pasta in a heated serving dish. Add sauce and toss. Top with caviar. Toss again at the table, taking care not to break the caviar eggs.

EGG NOODLES WITH SMOKED SALMON

This recipe can easily be doubled. For economy's sake, odd bits and ends of smoked salmon can be used. The dish must be made quickly.

2 TO 3 SERVINGS

3 tablespoons butter
4 ounces thinly sliced smoked salmon, chopped
2 tablespoons brandy
⅔ cup heavy cream
6 to 8 ounces thin egg noodles, freshly cooked al dente and drained
⅔ cup freshly grated Parmesan cheese or to taste
Freshly ground pepper
2 tablespoons minced fresh chives or dill (optional)

Melt the butter in a casserole that can go to the table and will hold all the ingredients. Add the salmon and cook over low heat, stirring all the time, for 2 minutes or just until the salmon loses its bright pink color. Add the brandy and flame if desired. Add the cream and heat through thoroughly but do not boil. Remove from heat, add the noodles, Parmesan and pepper and toss well. Heat through again and serve immediately, sprinkled with chives.

NOODLE- OR MACARONI-TUNAFISH CASSEROLE

When well made, this is a very good dish, bearing little resemblance to what school and college cafeterias serve. Increase the noodles or macaroni only if you absolutely must.

4 SERVINGS

3 tablespoons butter
3 tablespoons flour
2 cups milk
¾ cup shredded Swiss or Cheddar cheese
Salt
Freshly ground pepper
1 can (13 ounces) white meat tuna, drained and flaked
4 ounces medium noodles or elbow macaroni, cooked al dente and drained
3 tablespoons finely chopped pitted black or green olives or minced parsley
½ cup fine dry breadcrumbs blended with 2 tablespoons (¼ stick) butter, melted

Melt the butter in a heavy saucepan, stir in the flour and cook over low heat, stirring constantly, for about 1 minute. Whisk in the milk and cook, stirring all the time, for about 4 to 5 minutes or until the sauce is smooth and thick and has lost the raw flour taste. Stir in the cheese and cook, stirring, just until melted. Season with salt and pepper. Remove from heat and reserve. Combine the tuna, noodles, olives and cheese sauce in a large bowl and toss well with two forks. Spoon lightly into a generously buttered 2-quart casserole. Top with buttered breadcrumbs. Bake uncovered in a preheated 350°F oven for 20 to 30 minutes or until golden brown and bubbly. Serve hot.

VARIATION
Add 1 cup chopped cooked ham and/or ½ to 1 cup cooked peas; use a larger (about 2½-quart) casserole.

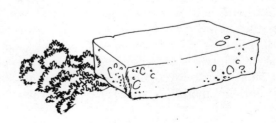

NOODLES WITH MUSSELS

2 TO 4 SERVINGS

3 pounds mussels
1½ cups dry white wine
2 tablespoons (¼ stick) butter and 2
    tablespoons olive oil, or 4 tablespoons olive
    oil
2 garlic cloves, minced
12 ounces thin or medium noodles
Salt
Freshly ground pepper
¼ cup minced parsley or cilantro

Scrub the mussels, remove beards and soak in cold water to cover for 15 minutes. Drain; discard any opened mussels. Transfer mussels to a large pot and add the wine. Cover and cook over high heat for 4 to 5 minutes or until mussels have opened. Drain and reserve mussels. Strain cooking liquid through a fine sieve lined with dampened cheesecloth or paper coffee filter. When the mussels are cool enough to handle, discard shells. Heat the butter and oil in a large deep frying pan. Add the garlic and cook for 2 to 3 minutes. Add the strained mussel liquid and boil over high heat until reduced to about ¾ cup. Add the shelled mussels, cover the pan and keep warm over lowest possible heat.

While mussels are cooking, cook the noodles in plenty of rapidly boiling salted water until al dente. Drain and turn into a heated serving dish. Season with a little salt and pepper. Top with the mussels and their liquid. Sprinkle with parsley and serve immediately, tossing at the table.

• • •

PARTY SEAFOOD LASAGNE

You can use one pound of sea scallops for this delicate dish instead of the bay scallops; quarter sea scallops before rinsing and drying. You may also prepare the dish in the morning, refrigerate it (covered with plastic wrap) until evening and bake it then. Baking time for the refrigerated dish will be about 20 to 25 minutes longer. Freezing is possible but not advisable, since the delicate shellfish tends to get mushy and the sauce may separate. If you freeze it, bring the lasagne back to room temperature before baking to help keep the fish firm.

8 SERVINGS

4 cups water
Salt
1 teaspoon sugar
8 whole peppercorns
1 pound medium shrimp, in their shells
1 pound bay scallops, rinsed and patted dry
8 flat or curly lasagne noodles (about 6
    ounces)

1 tablespoon oil
½ cup (1 stick) butter
½ cup minced green onions, white part only
½ cup flour
2 cups half-and-half or milk
2 tablespoons tomato paste
⅛ teaspoon cayenne pepper
2 tablespoons brandy
1¼ cups freshly grated Parmesan cheese

Combine water, 2 teaspoons salt, sugar and peppercorns in a large saucepan and bring to the boiling point. Add the shrimp and scallops, return to boil and cook for about 1 minute or just until the shrimp turns pink and scallops are tender (do not overcook). Drain, reserving the broth and peppercorns. Set the scallops aside. Peel shrimp, reserving shells. Devein shrimp and halve crosswise, then cut again into halves lengthwise. Combine the shrimp and scallops. Return the reserved broth to the saucepan, adding the peppercorns and shrimp shells. Boil the mixture over high heat for 15 to 20 minutes or until it is reduced to about 2 to 2½ cups of broth. Strain broth, discarding shells and peppercorns. Set aside 2 cups of strained broth.

Bring 3 quarts of water to boil in a large pot. Add 1 tablespoon salt. Gradually add lasagne noodles so that the water continues to boil rapidly. Cook noodles about 5 to 7 minutes, or until barely tender, stirring once or twice; do not overcook. Drain noodles, rinse in cold water and drain again. Return noodles to pot. Toss gently with oil to prevent noodles from sticking; set aside.

Melt butter in large saucepan, add green onions and cook over medium heat about 3 to 5 minutes, or until tender, stirring constantly. Reduce heat to low, add flour and cook, stirring until bubbly, then cook 1 minute longer, stirring constantly. Gradually add reserved 2 cups broth and the half-and-half. Stir or whisk over medium-low heat until mixture comes to boil and is thickened and smooth. Reduce heat to very low. Add tomato paste and cayenne and stir or whisk just until tomato paste is well blended into sauce. Taste and salt if necessary. Stir in brandy. Remove from heat. Stir in reserved cooked shrimp and scallops; you will have about 6 cups sauce.

Line bottom of a buttered 13×9×2-inch baking pan with 4 lasagne noodles, cutting one noodle as necessary so that bottom is completely covered. Spread evenly with half of shrimp-scallop sauce (about 3 cups). Sprinkle evenly with ½ cup Parmesan cheese. Top with remaining 4 noodles, cutting one noodle so that shrimp-scallop mixture is completely covered. Carefully and evenly spread on remaining shrimp-scallop sauce. Sprinkle with remaining ¾ cup cheese. Bake in a preheated 350° oven about 45 minutes, or until lasagne is hot and bubbly and top is lightly browned. Remove from oven and let stand 15 minutes. Cut in squares and serve on heated plates.

Pasta with Striped Bass Sauce

A popular sauce that can be made with other fish fillets as well.

ABOUT 2½ CUPS SAUCE;
4 TO 6 SERVINGS

- 2 tablespoons vegetable or olive oil
- 1 garlic clove, minced
- 2 tablespoons minced parsley
- 1 tablespoon minced fresh basil or 1 teaspoon dried
- 1 tablespoon minced fresh dill
- 4 medium-size ripe tomatoes, peeled and chopped
- ½ cup dry white wine
- 1½ pounds fresh bass or other fish fillets, cut into 1-inch pieces

Salt

Freshly ground pepper

- 12 to 16 ounces thin spaghetti, freshly cooked al dente and drained

Heat the oil in a deep large frying pan over medium heat. Add garlic, parsley, basil, and dill and cook for 2 minutes. Add the tomatoes and wine and simmer uncovered over low heat for about 10 minutes or until thickened. Add fish and simmer for 5 to 7 minutes or just until fish is cooked through. Serve immediately over freshly cooked pasta.

Spaghetti with Swordfish in Tomato Sauce

ABOUT 2⅓ CUPS SAUCE;
4 SERVINGS

- 2 pounds swordfish
- ¼ cup olive or vegetable oil
- 2 tablespoons (¼ stick) butter
- 1 cup minced parsley
- 2 garlic cloves, minced
- 2 cups plain tomato sauce
- 2 tablespoons fresh lemon juice
- 1 tablespoon fennel seed

Salt

Freshly ground pepper

- 1 pound spaghetti, freshly cooked al dente and drained
- ½ cup minced pitted black imported olives

Preheat the oven to 400°F. Cut the swordfish into bite-size pieces; remove all skin and bones. Place in one layer in a buttered baking dish. Heat oil and butter in a medium saucepan. Add the parsley and garlic and cook over medium heat, stirring constantly, for about 5 minutes. Add the tomato sauce, lemon juice, and fennel seed. Season with salt and pepper. Cook, stirring constantly for 5 minutes or until heated through. Pour sauce over the fish and bake for about 15 to 20 minutes or until the fish flakes. Turn the hot pasta into a heated serving dish. Spoon fish and sauce over it and sprinkle with the olives. Serve immediately.

Note: For a thinner sauce, use about 3 cups tomato sauce or to taste.

Pasta with Meat

Austrian Veal Goulash à la Richard Strauss

Family "One-Pot" Macaroni Dinner

About Lasagne

Baked Lasagne

Baked Ziti

Lasagne Pasticciate

Nona's Lamb and Spinach Curry

Oriental Green Peppers and Beef

Pastitsio

Penne alla Furiosa

Quiche Lorraine in a Noodle Shell

Quick Hamburger Stroganoff on Noodles

Schinkenfleckerln

Simple Macaroni Cheese and Ham Puff

Sour Cream Noodle Casserole

Spaghetti all' Amatriciana

Spaghetti and Meat Balls

Classic Spaghetti and Meat Balls

Spaghetti Carbonara

Tortellini with Cream

Tortellini Timbale

Austrian Veal Goulash à la Richard Strauss

This was, according to his wife as told to my mother, the favorite dish of the composer of Rosenkavalier, Salome, Electra etc. He particularly liked the goulash with buttered noodles.

4 TO 6 SERVINGS

1½ to 2 pounds boneless veal
Salt
Freshly ground pepper
 ¼ cup (½ stick) unsalted butter
 2 medium onions, thinly sliced
 2 large tomatoes, peeled and coarsely chopped
1½ tablespoons flour
 ⅔ cup dry white wine
 ½ cup sour cream
 ¼ cup (or more) hot beef bouillon
Juice of ½ lemon
 2 teaspoons caraway seed
Sweet paprika
12 to 16 ounces medium noodles, freshly cooked al dente, drained and tossed with 2 tablespoons (¼ stick) butter

Cut the meat into 1½-inch squares and trim off all fat and gristle. Season with salt and pepper. Melt the butter in a large saucepan. Add the meat and cook, over high heat, stirring constantly, for about 5 minutes or until golden brown. Add the onions and tomatoes and cook over medium heat, stirring frequently, until pan juices have almost entirely evaporated. Sprinkle the flour over the meat and cook for 1 to 2 minutes. Add the wine, sour cream, ¼ cup bouillon, lemon juice, caraway seed and a sprinkling of paprika. Cover tightly and simmer over low heat for about 45 minutes or until the meat is tender. Check frequently; if the dish is too dry, add a little more bouillon. Serve as is with buttered noodles or, for a finer dish, remove the meat with a slotted spoon and strain the sauce. Return meat to saucepan with sauce and heat through.

• • •

Family "One-Pot" Macaroni Dinner

4 SERVINGS

8 ounces ground beef
3 tablespoons butter, margarine or vegetable oil
2 large onions, quartered, then very thinly sliced (about 2 cups)
1 large garlic clove, minced
1 can (13¾ ounces) beef bouillon, undiluted

1 can (16 ounces) tomatoes, chopped, with
 their juice
Salt (optional)
Freshly ground pepper
4 ounces elbow macaroni
Freshly grated Parmesan, Cheddar, or Swiss
cheese

Brown the beef in a heavy large frying pan,
stirring frequently with two forks to break up
lumps. Drain off any fat and remove beef from
the pan; reserve. In the same frying pan melt
the butter, add the onions and garlic and cook
over medium heat, stirring frequently, for about
7 minutes or until tender. Add the beef, the
beef bouillon and the tomatoes. Check the seasoning; if necessary, add salt (bouillon will be
salty) and pepper. Bring to the boiling point and
stir in the uncooked macaroni. Reduce heat to
very low and simmer uncovered, stirring frequently, for about 15 minutes or until macaroni
is tender and most of the liquid has been absorbed. Serve immediately with grated cheese,
or if desired, sprinkle with about 1 cup cheese
and let stand for 2 to 3 minutes or until the
cheese has melted.

ABOUT LASAGNE

If you don't find it worthwhile to prepare lasagne for only four people, make it for eight but
bake it in two pans, each to serve four; freeze
the second pan. I use 8×8×2-inch baking pans,
each with a two-quart volume; the volume must
be kept in mind when choosing the pans. You
may use differently shaped pans, but they must
hold two quarts; depending on the shape, more
noodles may be needed to make two layers.
Another convenience is disposable foil pans such
as 7⅞ × 7⅛ × 1¾-inch square cake pans. Before
using them, turn the rolled rim of the pan upward so that the depth will measure two inches.
 When glass baking dishes are used, reduce the
oven temperature from 375°F to 350°F.

Reheating Frozen Lasagne and Other
Stuffed Pasta

Though lasagne or other stuffed pasta is always
better freshly made than reheated, there are
times when assembling the dish ahead and
freezing it is the only practical course.
 For best results, frozen lasagne and other
stuffed pasta should be partially thawed before
being put into the oven to reheat. Do this by
taking the hard-frozen dish out of the freezer
the evening before serving it; store in the refrigerator until baking time. The time required to
reheat a frozen and partly thawed stuffed pasta
dish will vary depending on how frozen the

pasta is, the type of filling, the size of the casserole and the oven temperature. It may be as little as 30 minutes or as much as 1½ hours, or until the center of the dish is thoroughly hot and the top golden brown. The oven temperature should be moderate—350°F to 375°F—to allow the pasta to heat through without burning on the outside.

Since reheating dries out frozen foods, partial thawing in the refrigerator will help keep the stuffed pasta dish nice and moist. Another aid to preserving moistness is to cover the pasta with aluminum foil for half of the baking time, then remove it to finish baking.

If you must reheat the pasta straight from the freezer, proceed as above, but baking time will be longer than for a partly thawed dish. Try keeping hard-frozen stuffed pasta covered with aluminum foil for ⅔ of the baking time; remove the foil for the last third of baking time. Depending on size or kind of the straight-from-freezer-dish, you may also have to reheat it at a lower temperature, such as 300°F.

Remember that dishes made with a cream sauce ideally should not be frozen. If freeze you must, cook or bake dishes with cream sauce first, cool thoroughly, wrap tightly and then freeze.

Lasagne and other stuffed pasta dishes that contain no cream sauce freeze better. I find it preferable not to cook or bake them before freezing; just assemble the dish, wrap and freeze.

BAKED LASAGNE

ABOUT 4½ TO 5 CUPS SAUCE;
6 TO 8 SERVINGS

12 ounces ground beef
3 tablespoons oil, preferably olive
1 large onion, chopped (1 cup)
2 large garlic cloves, minced
1 can (28 ounces) tomatoes, preferably Italian style, pureed in food processor or blender until smooth
1 can (6 ounces) tomato paste
⅓ cup water
1½ teaspoons dried basil
1 teaspoon oregano
1 teaspoon sugar (optional)
Salt
¼ teaspoon freshly ground pepper
1 bay leaf, broken in half
2 cups (1 pound) fresh whole or skim milk ricotta or one 15-ounce container
¼ cup freshly grated Parmesan cheese
1 egg
½ teaspoon salt
¼ teaspoon freshly ground pepper
8 lasagne noodles (about 6 ounces)
1 tablespoon oil
½ cup freshly grated Parmesan cheese

Brown beef in a Dutch oven or other large pot, stirring occasionally to break up the meat. Drain off fat; remove meat and set aside. Heat 3 tablespoons oil in the same Dutch oven, add onion and garlic and cook over medium heat, stirring occasionally, about 5 to 8 minutes or until the onion is tender. Stir in the reserved meat, tomatoes, tomato paste, water, basil, oregano, sugar, ¾ teaspoon salt, ¼ teaspoon pepper and bay leaf and bring to boil. Cover and simmer, stirring occasionally, about 2 hours or until flavors are blended and mixture thickens slightly (there will be about 4½ to 5 cups sauce).

Combine ricotta, ¼ cup Parmesan, egg, ½ teaspoon salt and ¼ teaspoon pepper in a medium bowl; set aside.

Bring 3 quarts water to boil in a large pot. Add 1 tablespoon salt, then gradually add lasagne noodles so that water continues to boil. Cook noodles until barely tender, about 5 minutes, stirring once or twice; do not overcook. Drain noodles; rinse in cold water and drain well. Return noodles to pot. Toss gently with 1 tablespoon oil to prevent noodles from sticking. Line the bottom of a buttered 13×9×2-inch baking pan with 4 lasagne noodles, cutting one noodle as necessary so that the bottom is completely covered. Spread evenly with half of ricotta mixture (1 generous cup). Sprinkle evenly with half of the mozzarella cheese (about 2 cups). Spread with half of tomato meat mixture (about 2½ cups). Top with remaining 4 noodles, cutting one noodle as above so that tomato mixture is completely covered. Evenly layer on remaining half of ricotta mixture, remaining

mozzarella cheese and remaining tomato mixture. Sprinkle the top evenly with ½ cup Parmesan cheese. Bake in a preheated 375°F oven about 45 to 50 minutes or until lasagne is hot in center. Remove from oven; let stand 15 minutes. Cut in squares and serve on heated plates.

Note: Two smaller lasagne casseroles may be prepared if desired. Use 2 buttered 8×8×2-inch baking pans or 2 disposable foil 7⅞ × 7⅞ × 1¾-inch square cake pans. Turn rolled rim of foil pans upward so depth of pans will measure 2 inches. Use 9 lasagne noodles, about 7 ounces. Place 3 noodles side by side in one 8 × 8 × 2-inch baking pan, allowing noodles to come up sides of pan. Evenly layer on ¼ of mozzarella cheese, then ¼ of tomato mixture. Fold overlap of noodles over onto tomato layer (this will begin the second layer of noodles). Cover exposed tomato mixture with 3 half noodles. Evenly layer on ¼ of ricotta mixture, ¼ of mozzarella and ¼ cup Parmesan cheese. Repeat procedure for the second casserole. Wrap one casserole airtight and freeze. Bake remaining casserole uncovered in preheated 375°F oven about 45 minutes or until heated through. Let stand 15 minutes before serving. Each pan makes 4 servings.

———   · · ·   ———

BAKED ZITI

Follow directions for Baked Lasagne but substitute 12 ounces (about 4 cups) ziti for lasagne noodles. Cook ziti in 4 quarts boiling salted water until barely tender, about 5 minutes, stirring once or twice. Drain, rinse in cold water and drain well. In the layering procedure, layer ¼ of the cooked ziti (about 1½ cups) in place of ¼ of lasagne noodles for each casserole. Bake as for Baked Lasagne.

• • •

LASAGNE PASTICCIATE

A traditional dish.

8 SERVINGS

FILLING
11 tablespoons (1 stick plus 3 tablespoons) butter
1 tablespoon oil, preferably olive
8 ounces chicken livers, halved, trimmed (if necessary), and patted dry
1 large onion, minced (1 cup)
½ cup minced celery
¼ cup minced carrot
4 ounces prosciutto or smoked ham, minced
4 ounces *each* ground beef round and lean ground pork
1 cup dry white wine
½ cup beef bouillon
2 tablespoons tomato paste
½ teaspoon freshly ground pepper

BECHAMEL SAUCE
½ cup flour
4 cups milk
¾ teaspoon salt
⅛ teaspoon freshly ground pepper
⅛ teaspoon freshly grated nutmeg
8 lasagne noodles (about 6 ounces)
1 tablespoon oil
1½ cups freshly grated Parmesan cheese

For filling: Melt 1 tablespoon butter and 1 tablespoon oil in heavy large frying pan until the butter is bubbly. Add the chicken livers and cook over medium-high heat about 5 to 7 minutes until livers are nicely browned, turning occasionally and reducing heat slightly if necessary. Transfer livers to large bowl. Using kitchen shears, cut livers into small pieces; set aside. Add 2 tablespoons butter to drippings in frying pan and heat until bubbly. Add onion, celery, carrot and prosciutto and cook over medium heat about 5 to 7 minutes until the vegetables are tender, stirring frequently. Add vegetable mixture to the livers. In the same frying pan, brown beef and pork over medium-high heat, stirring occasionally to break up meat. Add the wine and cook over high heat until almost completely evaporated, about 10 minutes. Add liver mixture to beef mixture with bouillon, tomato paste and ½ teaspoon pepper. Simmer uncovered until flavors are nicely blended, about 15 minutes, stirring occasionally (there will be about 3 cups).

For bechamel sauce: Melt the remaining 8 table-spoons butter in a large saucepan. Stir in the flour and cook and stir over medium heat until smooth, about 1 to 2 minutes. Reduce heat to low and stir in the milk. Cook, stirring constantly, until the mixture thickens and comes to the boiling point. Stir in ¾ teaspoon salt, ⅛ teaspoon pepper and the nutmeg (makes about 4 cups).

Bring 3 quarts water to boil in large pot. Add 1 tablespoon salt, then gradually add lasagne noodles so that water continues to boil. Cook noodles about 5 minutes or until barely tender,

stirring once or twice; do not overcook. Drain noodles, rinse in cold water and drain well. Return noodles to pot. Toss gently with 1 table-spoon oil to prevent noodles from sticking. Line the bottom of a buttered 13×9×2-inch baking pan with 4 lasagne noodles, cutting one noodle as necessary so that bottom of pan is completely covered. Spread evenly with one-half the liver mixture (about 1½ cups). Sprinkle evenly with ½ cup Parmesan cheese. Carefully and evenly spread with one-half the bechamel sauce (about 2 cups). Top with remaining 4 noodles, cutting one noodle as above so that bechamel is completely covered. Spread evenly with the remaining liver mixture. Sprinkle with ½ cup Parmesan cheese, then spread on the remaining bechamel. Sprinkle the top evenly with the remaining ½ cup cheese. Bake in preheated 375°F oven about 40 minutes, or until lasagne is hot and bubbly and top is lightly browned. Remove from the oven; let stand 15 minutes. Cut in squares and serve on heated plates.

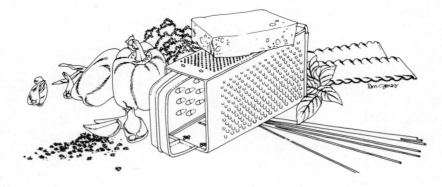

NONA'S LAMB AND SPINACH CURRY

Serve on Chinese or Japanese egg or buckwheat noodles, or on thin fettucine.

6 SERVINGS

¼ cup (½ stick) butter
2 large onions, minced
1 one-inch piece fresh ginger, minced (about 1 tablespoon)
3 garlic cloves, minced
3 tablespoons curry powder
2 pounds lean lamb, trimmed of all fat and cut into 1½-inch pieces
¼ cup plain yogurt
1 teaspoon hot pepper sauce (omit if curry powder is hot)
1 teaspoon salt
3 packages frozen spinach (10 ounces each), thawed or 1½ pounds fresh spinach, blanched and pressed dry
½ teaspoon freshly grated nutmeg
1 pound Chinese or Japanese buckwheat noodles, freshly cooked, drained

Melt the butter in a heavy large frying pan. Add the onions, ginger and garlic and cook over medium heat, stirring constantly, until the onion begins to brown. Stir in curry powder and cook for 2 more minutes. Add the lamb and cook, stirring constantly, for 6 to 10 minutes or until browned on all sides. Stir in yogurt, hot pepper sauce and salt. Remove from heat and keep warm. With hands, squeeze moisture out of the thawed frozen spinach or blanched fresh spinach until it is about half its original volume. Add to meat mixture and mix well. Place over low heat, cover and simmer for about 1 hour, or until the meat is cooked through and the spinach is cooked down to a thin paste. Stir frequently and, if necessary to prevent scorching, add a little hot water during cooking. Stir in nutmeg. Turn noodles into a heated serving dish and pour the lamb and spinach curry over noodles. Toss at the table and serve hot.

ORIENTAL GREEN PEPPERS AND BEEF

Transparent noodles must be soaked for 20 minutes in cold water and drained before being added to any dish. It is best to cut the soaked drained noodles with a pair of kitchen scissors into manageable 6- to 8-inch strands. Freshly cooked, thin Chinese noodles, thin egg noodles or spaghettini can also be used for this dish.

4 TO 6 SERVINGS

½ cup imported dried mushrooms or Chinese mushrooms
6 tablespoons vegetable oil
2 medium onions, halved and thinly sliced
2 garlic cloves, minced
1 tablespoon minced fresh ginger or to taste
1½ pounds boneless lean tender beef, cut into 2 × ½-inch strips
4 sweet green peppers, seeded and cut into 1-inch squares
1 tablespoon soy sauce
1 teaspoon ground aniseed (optional)
Salt
Freshly ground pepper
8 ounces snow peas, blanched*
8 ounces cellophane noodles (bean threads), soaked and drained

*To blanch snow peas, cover with boiling water and let stand 3 minutes; drain well.

Rinse the mushrooms under cold running water and place in a small bowl. Cover with water and let stand for at least 15 minutes. Drain. Trim mushrooms, discarding tough stems. If large, cut into halves or quarters. Heat the oil in a deep large frying pan over medium-high heat. Add the onions, garlic, and ginger and cook, stirring constantly, for 2 to 3 minutes. Add the meat and cook over high heat, stirring constantly, for 5 minutes. Reduce heat to low. Add green peppers, soy sauce, aniseed, a little salt, and pepper. Mix well, cover and cook over low heat for about 10 minutes. Add the snow peas and mushrooms and cook for 3 to 5 minutes. Serve over noodles.

PASTITSIO

8 SERVINGS

1½ pounds lean ground beef
¼ cup (½ stick) butter or margarine
3 large onions, chopped (3 cups)
3 large garlic cloves, minced
1 can (28 ounces) tomatoes, preferably Italian style, coarsely chopped
1 can (6 ounces) tomato paste
⅓ cup water
Salt
1 teaspoon sugar
1 teaspoon dried basil
½ teaspoon oregano
¼ teaspoon freshly ground pepper or to taste
⅛ teaspoon (generous) cinnamon
12 ounces elbow macaroni (3 cups)
¾ cup freshly grated Parmesan cheese or 12 ounces feta cheese, shredded
Custard Sauce (see recipe)

Brown the beef in a Dutch oven or other large pot, stirring occasionally to break up meat. Drain off the fat; set meat aside. Melt the butter in the same Dutch oven, add onions and garlic and cook over medium heat, stirring occasionally, about 8 to 10 minutes until onion is tender. Stir in beef, tomatoes, tomato paste, water, 1½ teaspoons salt, sugar, basil, oregano, pepper and cinnamon. Bring to boil. Reduce heat, cover and simmer, stirring occasionally, until slightly thickened, about 45 minutes (there will be about 6½ cups). Meanwhile, bring 4 to 6 quarts water to boil in large pot. Add 1 tablespoon salt, then gradually add macaroni so that water continues to boil. Cook 3 to 5 minutes until barely tender, stirring once or twice; do not overcook. Drain macaroni, rinse in cold water and drain well. Toss with ½ teaspoon salt.

Evenly spread ¼ of macaroni (about 1½ cups) in lightly greased 8×8×2-inch baking pan. Evenly and carefully spread with half of meat sauce (about 3¼ cups). Layer on ¼ of macaroni (1½ cups). Sprinkle evenly with 3 tablespoons Parmesan or 3 ounces (about 1 cup) feta cheese. Repeat procedure in second 8×8×2-inch pan. Bake both casseroles in preheated 350°F oven for 20 minutes. Evenly spread half the custard sauce (about 1¾ cups) on each casserole. Sprinkle each evenly with 3 tablespoons Parmesan or about 1 cup feta cheese. Bake another 25 to 30 minutes or until knife inserted in custard comes out clean. Cool 20 minutes, then cut into squares and serve on heated plates.

CUSTARD SAUCE

3 eggs
⅓ cup butter
⅓ cup flour
3 cups milk
¾ teaspoon salt
⅛ teaspoon (generous) freshly grated nutmeg
⅛ teaspoon freshly ground pepper

Beat eggs well in large bowl; set aside. Melt butter in heavy large saucepan over medium heat. Add flour and cook, stirring, until bubbly. Add milk and stir or whisk until thickened and smooth, then simmer, stirring constantly, 5 minutes. Blend in seasonings. Remove from heat and whisk into beaten eggs.

PENNE ALLA FURIOSA

Penne or another short, thick pasta is best suited to this "furious" Roman dish, so called because it is highly spiced.

ABOUT 3½ CUPS SAUCE;
4 TO 6 SERVINGS

8 ounces pancetta or lean salt pork
1 tablespoon olive oil
1 medium onion, minced
2 to 4 garlic cloves, minced
6 anchovies, drained and minced or 2 tablespoons anchovy paste
2 pounds ripe tomatoes, peeled and chopped
1 to 2 teaspoons dried hot pepper flakes or to taste
Salt (optional)
12 to 16 ounces penne
1 cup freshly grated Parmesan or Romano cheese

Blanch pancetta or salt pork by covering with boiling water; let stand for 3 minutes. Drain well and pat dry with paper towels. Cut into small dice. Combine olive oil, pancetta, onion and garlic in a deep large frying pan and cook over medium-low heat, stirring constantly, for about 5 to 7 minutes or until onion is opaque and begins to turn golden. Stir in anchovies. Add tomatoes, hot pepper, and (if needed) salt to taste. Cook over high heat, stirring constantly, for about 3 minutes. Reduce heat to low and simmer uncovered for about 15 minutes, or until sauce is the consistency of thick tomato sauce.

While the sauce is cooking, cook the pasta in plenty of rapidly boiling salted water until al dente. Drain and return to cooking pot. Pour half of the sauce and half of the cheese over the pasta and toss well. Turn into a heated serving dish and top with remaining sauce and cheese. Serve immediately.

QUICHE LORRAINE IN A NOODLE SHELL

A noodle rather than a pastry shell makes for a welcome change in any kind of quiche.

4 SERVINGS

6 ounces fine noodles
10 slices bacon
4 eggs
1½ cups shredded Gruyère or Swiss cheese
1⅓ cups milk, half-and-half, or milk and heavy cream, mixed
⅛ teaspoon freshly grated nutmeg
Salt (optional)
Freshly ground pepper
3 to 4 tablespoons butter

Cook the noodles in plenty of boiling water until almost but not quite al dente; noodles will cook further with filling. Drain. Butter a deep 10-inch pie dish and line bottom with the noodles.

Fry the bacon until very crisp; drain on paper towels and crumble. Beat the eggs in a large bowl. Blend in the cheese, milk, nutmeg and crumbled bacon. Season with salt (if necessary) and pepper. Pour mixture onto the noodles, distributing evenly. Dot with butter. Bake in preheated 375°F oven for about 30 minutes or until set and golden brown. Serve immediately.

Note: For a thinner noodle shell, use 4 ounces fine noodles.

QUICK HAMBURGER STROGANOFF ON NOODLES

A pleasant, inexpensive version of the more elegant Beef Stroganoff.

3 TO 4 SERVINGS

1 tablespoon butter or vegetable oil
1 medium onion, minced
1 pound lean ground beef
4 ounces mushrooms, thinly sliced or 1 can (6 ounces) sliced mushrooms
1 tablespoon flour
Salt
Freshly ground pepper
2 tablespoons tomato ketchup or chili sauce
1½ cups sour cream or equal parts sour cream and plain yogurt
6 to 8 ounces medium noodles, freshly cooked al dente and drained
2 tablespoons minced parsley, chives, or dill

Melt the butter in a deep large frying pan over medium heat. Add the onion and cook until soft; do not brown. Add beef and mushrooms and cook over medium heat, stirring constantly with a fork, until meat is browned on the outside but still pinkish inside (or cook to desired doneness). Drain off fat. Stir in flour, salt, and pepper and mix well. Stir in ketchup and cook, stirring constantly, for 2 minutes or until mixture thickens. Blend in sour cream and heat through but do not boil. Turn noodles into a heated serving dish, top with meat mixture and sprinkle with parsley. Serve immediately, tossing at the table.

. . .

SCHINKENFLECKERLN

An Austrian ham and noodle casserole that makes a good buffet dish. Traditionally, this dish is made with little noodle squares available in Hungarian and Czech groceries. Wide noodles will also serve, but they should be broken into 1½-inch pieces before cooking.

6 SERVINGS

1 pound wide noodles, broken into 1½-inch pieces
1 pound lean cooked ham, cut into ½-inch pieces
¾ cup (1½ sticks) butter, at room temperature
6 eggs, separated
1½ cups sour cream
Salt
Freshly ground pepper

Cook the noodles in plenty of rapidly boiling salted water until not quite al dente. Drain and transfer to a large bowl. Add the ham and toss with 2 forks. Cream the butter in another bowl. Beat in egg yolks one at a time, blending well after each addition. Beat in sour cream (the longer the mixture is beaten, the lighter the dish). Add to noodle mixture and blend well. Season with salt and pepper. Beat the egg whites until stiff and fold into the ham mixture. Spoon into a buttered 3-quart baking dish that can go to the table. Bake in preheated 350°F oven for about 25 minutes or until crisp and golden. Serve immediately.

SIMPLE MACARONI, CHEESE AND HAM PUFF

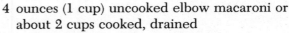
4 SERVINGS

4 ounces (1 cup) uncooked elbow macaroni or
 about 2 cups cooked, drained
1 cup grated Cheddar or Swiss cheese
½ cup ground cooked ham
¼ cup minced parsley or chives
Salt
Freshly ground pepper
3 eggs, separated

Cook macaroni in plenty of rapidly boiling salted water until al dente; drain. Combine macaroni with cheese, ham, parsley, salt (be careful;
cheese and ham are salty) and pepper and mix
well. Beat egg yolks and stir into mixture. Beat
the whites until stiff but not dry and fold carefully into the macaroni mixture. Spoon mixture
into generously buttered 6-cup baking dish;
smooth the top. Bake in a preheated 350°F oven
for about 25 minutes or until golden and puffy.
Serve hot.

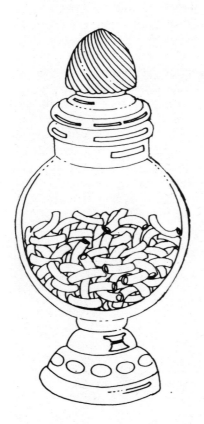

Sour Cream Noodle Casserole

I have a friend who often takes this dish to pot luck suppers; she gets raves every time.

MAKES 2 CASSEROLES OF 4 SERVINGS EACH

2 pounds lean ground beef
2 tablespoons *each* butter or margarine and oil
5 medium onions, chopped (2½ cups)
1 large garlic clove, minced
8 ounces mushrooms, thinly sliced (about 2½ cups)
1 can (15 ounces) tomato sauce
1 can (6 ounces) tomato paste
2 tablespoons sugar
Salt
¾ teaspoon freshly ground pepper
8 ounces medium egg noodles (about 6½ cups)
1 cup sour cream
8 ounces mozzarella cheese, shredded

Brown the beef in a Dutch oven or other large pot, breaking up meat with a fork. Drain off fat and remove beef from the pot. Heat butter and oil in the same Dutch oven. Add the onions and garlic and cook over medium heat until onions are almost tender, about 5 minutes, stirring occasionally. Add mushrooms and cook, stirring until onions and mushrooms are tender, about 5 more minutes. Stir in the beef, tomato sauce, tomato paste, sugar, 1½ teaspoons salt and pepper. Bring to boil, stirring constantly, then remove from the heat (there will be about 6 cups sauce).

Bring 3 quarts water to boil in large pot. Add 1 tablespoon salt, then gradually add noodles so that water continues to boil. Cook until the noodles are barely tender, about 3 minutes, stirring once or twice; do not overcook. Drain, rinse with cold water and drain well. Place ¼ of the noodles (about 1½ cups) in greased 2-quart casserole or 8×8×2-inch pan. Spoon ¼ cup sour cream in small dollops over noodle layer. Cover evenly with ¼ of the meat sauce (about 1½ cups). Repeat layering, ending with meat sauce. Sprinkle with half of the mozzarella (about 1¼ cups). Repeat the procedure to make second casserole of same size. Bake in preheated 350°F oven for glass dish or preheated 375°F oven for metal or foil pan about 35 to 40 minutes or until the center is hot. (If desired, bake just one casserole; wrap the other airtight and freeze.)

Note: Disposable foil 7⅞ × 7⅞ × 1¾-inch square cake pans can be used.

SPAGHETTI ALL'AMATRICIANA

This Roman specialty must be made with pancetta, lard, and plenty of pepper for an authentic "hefty" taste.

ABOUT 4 CUPS SAUCE;
4 to 6 SERVINGS

8 ounces pancetta, blanched and diced small (see page 18)
2 tablespoons lard
1 medium onion, thinly sliced
3½ pounds plum tomatoes, chopped or 3 cans (28 ounces each) plum tomatoes, well drained and chopped
Salt (optional)
¾ to 1 teaspoon freshly ground pepper
¼ teaspoon dried hot pepper flakes or to taste (optional)
1 pound spaghetti
⅔ cup freshly grated Romano cheese
⅔ cup freshly grated Parmesan cheese

Combine pancetta and lard in a deep large frying pan or saucepan and cook over low heat, stirring constantly for about 10 minutes or until the onion is soft. Add tomatoes, salt if needed, pepper and hot pepper flakes and cook over high heat, stirring constantly, for about 5 minutes or until the tomatoes are soft and just cooked; they must retain their shape. Cook spaghetti in plenty of rapidly boiling salted water until al dente; drain. Turn into a heated serving dish, add sauce and toss. Sprinkle with cheeses and serve immediately.

— · · · —

SPAGHETTI AND MEATBALLS
4 TO 6 SERVINGS

1 pound ground beef chuck
1 egg, beaten
1 garlic clove, minced
1 teaspoon salt
¼ teaspoon freshly ground pepper
¼ teaspoon oregano
2 tablespoons vegetable oil
1 can (8 ounces) tomato sauce
½ cup sour cream
Salt
Freshly ground pepper
1 tablespoon salt
3 quarts boiling water
8 ounces spaghetti

Combine beef, egg, garlic, 1 teaspoon salt, ¼ teaspoon pepper, and oregano and mix well. Shape into 2-inch balls. Heat oil in large frying pan. Add meatballs and cook over low heat until browned on all sides. Blend tomato sauce, sour cream, salt, and pepper. Pour over meatballs, cover and cook over low heat 10 minutes.

Meanwhile, add 1 tablespoon salt to rapidly boiling water. Gradually add spaghetti so that water continues to boil. Cook, uncovered, stirring occasionally, until al dente. Drain in colander. Top with meatballs and sauce and serve.

· · ·

CLASSIC SPAGHETTI AND MEATBALLS
12 SERVINGS

3 tablespoons olive or vegetable oil
6 garlic cloves, minced
¾ cup chopped parsley
3 cans (28 ounces each) plum tomatoes
3 cans (6 ounces each) tomato paste
1½ cups water
1 tablespoon sugar
1½ tablespoons salt
¾ teaspoon freshly ground pepper
¾ teaspoon dried basil
3 pounds lean ground beef
1 garlic clove, minced
3 tablespoons chopped parsley
1 tablespoon salt
¼ teaspoon freshly ground pepper
3 eggs
3 slices bread, softened in hot water, squeezed dry, and torn into small pieces
¾ cup freshly grated Parmesan cheese
⅓ cup olive oil or vegetable oil
3 tablespoons salt
6 to 9 quarts boiling water
1½ pounds spaghetti
Freshly grated Parmesan cheese

Heat oil in large kettle or Dutch oven over medium-high heat. Add 6 garlic cloves and ¾ cup parsley and sauté briefly. Stir in tomatoes, tomato paste, 1½ cups water, sugar, 1½ tablespoons salt, ¾ teaspoon pepper and basil. Cover and simmer 2 hours, stirring occasionally.

Combine beef, 1 garlic clove, 3 tablespoons parsley, 1 tablespoon salt, ¼ teaspoon pepper, eggs, bread and ¾ cup Parmesan cheese; mix well. Shape into 36 balls and brown in ⅓ cup oil. Add to spaghetti sauce for last 45 minutes cooking time.

Add 3 tablespoons salt to rapidly boiling water. Gradually add spaghetti so that water continues to boil. Cook, stirring occasionally, until al dente. Drain in colander. Top with meatballs and sauce, sprinkle with Parmesan cheese, and serve.

SPAGHETTI CARBONARA

A Roman dish that enchants foreigners. Speed is of the essence in preparing it since it must be served and eaten very hot. Lukewarm, the dish loses its character.

ABOUT 1²⁄₃ CUPS SAUCE;
4 SERVINGS

12 to 16 ounces spaghetti or linguine
 8 slices very lean bacon, minced
 2 tablespoons (¼ stick) butter
 1 small onion, minced
⅔ cup dry white wine
 3 eggs
⅔ cup freshly grated Parmesan cheese
¼ cup minced parsley
¼ teaspoon salt
¼ teaspoon freshly ground pepper
Freshly grated Parmesan cheese

Start cooking the spaghetti in plenty of rapidly boiling salted water so that it is ready by the time you finish the sauce. Combine the bacon and butter in a saucepan and heat. Add onion and cook, stirring constantly, until soft. Stir in the wine and cook over high heat, stirring constantly, until evaporated. Remove from direct heat, cover and keep as hot as possible over a flame guard or in a 250°F oven. In a very hot, deep serving dish beat the eggs with ⅔ cup cheese, parsley, salt, and pepper. Drain spaghet-ti, turn immediately into the dish with the egg mixture and toss well. Add the bacon mixture and toss again thoroughly, being sure the sauce coats all the pasta. Serve immediately with additional Parmesan cheese.

— · · · —

TORTELLINI WITH CREAM

Cooking small filled pastas in broth adds to their flavor. For cooking purposes, the broth does not have to be the finest; like most Italians, in this case I make mine with bouillon cubes.

4 TO 6 SERVINGS

2 quarts chicken bouillon
2 pounds fresh or frozen tortellini
2 cups heavy cream
1 teaspoon salt
¼ teaspoon hot pepper sauce or to taste
Freshly ground pepper
⅔ cup freshly grated Parmesan cheese
Additional freshly grated Parmesan cheese

Bring chicken bouillon to boil in a large deep saucepan. Add tortellini and cook for 5 to 7 minutes or until not quite tender (tortellini must be undercooked since they will be cooked again later). Drain and keep warm. Combine cream, salt, pepper sauce and ground pepper in a flameproof casserole that can go to the table and is big enough to hold all the ingredients. Bring to the boil; reduce heat to low. Add tortellini and cook uncovered for 5 more minutes or until tortellini are tender. Sprinkle with ⅔ cup Parmesan and serve immediately, with more Parmesan on the side.

VARIATION:
Cook 4 ounces sliced mushrooms in 2 tablespoons (¼ stick) butter for 3 to 4 minutes; mushrooms must remain firm. Add to cream with ½ cup julienne strips of ham or better, prosciutto. Add tortellini and proceed as directed.

--- • • • ---

TORTELLINI TIMBALE

An impressive but easy party dish which can be made with commercial frozen tortellini.

6 TO 8 SERVINGS

Butter
Fine dry breadcrumbs
1 cup (2 sticks) butter, cut into small pieces

3 pounds fresh tortellini or 3 packages (15 ounces each) frozen
2 cups freshly grated Parmesan cheese
Salt
Freshly ground pepper
⅛ teaspoon freshly grated nutmeg
Freshly grated Parmesan cheese
1 recipe Tomato Sauce (page 154)

Generously butter a straight-sided 12 cup mold such as a soufflé dish. Coat all surfaces with breadcrumbs. Cook tortellini in plenty of rapidly boiling salted water until amost but not quite tender (cooking time indicated on packages is usually too long; taste as pasta cooks). Drain thoroughly. Melt 1 cup butter in a large saucepan over low heat. Add tortellini and stir with a wooden spoon to coat with butter. Stir in the Parmesan, season with salt (Parmesan will be salty), pepper, and nutmeg, and mix well. Turn tortellini into prepared mold and press down with a wooden spoon to fill the mold evenly (mixture should be packed but not squashed; tortellini should keep their shape). Bake in a preheated 400°F oven for 15 minutes. Turn off oven and open door slightly; let stand in oven for 5 to 10 minutes (this will make unmolding easier). Unmold on a heated platter and sprinkle with a little Parmesan cheese. Drizzle a little tomato sauce in a star pattern over tortellini; serve remaining sauce on the side.

--- • • • ---

Pasta with Poultry

Cannelloni alla Nerone

Chicken and Mushroom Filled Manicotti

Chicken Tetrazzini

Church Supper Chicken, Noodle and
Spinach Casserole

Manicotti Imbottiti al Forno

Saffron Chicken on Noodles

Spaghetti alla Caruso

Cannelloni alla Nerone

A well-known New York restaurant dish from the thirties. Eat this freshly made; it does not freeze well.

MAKES 32 CANNELLONI,
ABOUT 8 SERVINGS

 2 medium whole boned skinned chicken breasts (about 1 pound), halved and trimmed of fat
 1 teaspoon salt
 ¼ teaspoon freshly ground black pepper
10 tablespoons (1¼ sticks) butter, divided
 2 tablespoons oil, preferably olive
 2 chicken livers (2 ounces), halved, trimmed (if necessary), and patted dry
 6 slices prosciutto (4 ounces)
1½ cups freshly grated Parmesan cheese, divided
 6 tablespoons flour
 3 cups milk
 1 cup heavy cream
 ½ teaspoon freshly ground white pepper
Basic Two-Egg Pasta (page 119)

Season both sides of the chicken breasts with ½ teaspoon salt and the black pepper. In a heavy large frying pan heat 2 tablespoons of the butter and the oil until the butter is bubbly. Add chicken and cook over medium-high heat about 15 to 20 minutes or until breasts are nicely browned and done, turning occasionally and reducing heat as necessary. Remove the breasts; cool. Add the chicken livers to the drippings in the frying pan and cook over medium heat, turning occasionally with 2 forks, until livers are nicely browned and tender, about 5 to 7 minutes. Transfer the livers to a food processor or grinder with the chicken breasts and prosciutto and grind finely. Stir in ½ cup Parmesan cheese; set aside. In a large saucepan melt the remaining 8 tablespoons of butter over medium-low heat. Add the flour and cook, stirring, until well blended and bubbly, about 2 to 3 minutes. Gradually stir in the milk and heavy cream. Cook and stir over low to medium heat until sauce thickens and comes to the boiling point. Stir in the remaining ½ teaspoon salt and the white pepper; mix well. Stir 1 cup sauce into the chicken mixture and mix well; chill while preparing the pasta (there will be 3 generous cups filling). Place waxed paper or plastic wrap directly on remaining sauce; chill.

Prepare Basic Two-Egg Pasta according to directions on page 119. Cover dough with a bowl and let it rest for 15 minutes. Cut dough into 2 equal portions. Cover one portion; shape the remaining dough into a ball. By hand or using machine roll dough into a ⅟₁₆-inch-thick strip about 27 to 30 inches long and 5½ inches wide, flouring as necessary. (If dough is rolled by hand, carefully lift strip when rolled ⅟₁₆ inch thick; lay back down on work surface without stretching it. This helps insure that dough is in a "relaxed" state, so it will be less likely to shrink when cut.)

With fluted pastry wheel or sharp knife cut strip into sixteen 2½-inch squares, rerolling scraps for some of the squares. (Pasta will expand during cooking.) As scraps are formed keep them covered to prevent drying; as the squares are cut, arrange on baking sheets lined with kitchen towels or waxed paper. Repeat with remaining half of dough making 16 additional 2½-inch squares. Drop half of pasta squares into 3 to 4 quarts boiling salted water; cover. When water returns to the boil, remove cover and cook, stirring once or twice, about 2 to 3 minutes, or until a small strip of dough cut off one square of pasta is tender but still al dente. With a slotted spoon quickly remove pasta from boiling water and arrange on damp kitchen towels. Repeat with remaining squares. Place squares on damp kitchen towels. Remove the plastic wrap or waxed paper from sauce and place over low heat just until heated through, stirring constantly. Evenly spread about 1 cup sauce on bottom of buttered 13×9×2-inch baking pan; keep remaining sauce warm. To form cannelloni, place a slightly rounded packed tablespoon of chicken filling in a strip along one edge of each pasta square (filling may "hang out" of the ends slightly, if desired). Roll to completely enclose filling. Arrange the filled cannelloni in a single layer seam side down atop sauce in the pan. Sprinkle evenly with ½ cup Parmesan cheese. Carefully spread remaining sauce (about 2 cups) on cannelloni. Sprinkle with remaining ½ cup cheese. Bake in preheated 375°F oven about 40 minutes, or until hot, bubbly and nicely browned on top. Let stand a few minutes before serving. Serve cannelloni on heated plates.

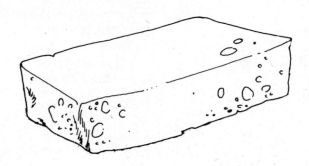

CHICKEN AND MUSHROOM FILLED MANICOTTI

6 SERVINGS

3 medium (about 1½ pounds), whole boned skinned chicken breasts, halved and trimmed of fat

2 teaspoons salt, divided

¾ teaspoon freshly ground pepper, divided

11 tablespoons (1 stick plus 3 tablespoons) butter, divided

3 tablespoons oil, preferably olive

8 ounces mushrooms, sliced

4 to 5 green onions with part tops, sliced (½ cup)

1 cup fresh breadcrumbs, preferably from Italian bread

2 eggs

6 tablespoons flour

3 cups milk

1 cup heavy cream

3 tablespoons dry Sherry

¼ teaspoon freshly grated nutmeg

1 to 2 tablespoons salt

16 manicotti noodles (one 8-ounce package contains 14 noodles)

1 cup freshly grated Parmesan cheese

½ cup sliced almonds

Season both sides of the chicken breasts with 1 teaspoon salt and ½ teaspoon pepper. In a heavy large frying pan heat 3 tablespoons butter and the oil until the butter is bubbly. Add the chicken breasts and cook over medium-high heat for about 15 minutes or until breasts are nicely browned and done, turning occasionally and reducing heat as necessary. Remove breasts; cool. Add mushrooms and green onions to fat remaining in the frying pan and cook over medium-high heat until mushrooms are tender, about 3 to 5 minutes, stirring occasionally. Increase the heat to high and boil briefly until mushroom liquid is almost cooked away. Combine chicken breasts and mushroom mixture in food processor or grinder and grind finely. Transfer to a bowl with breadcrumbs, remaining ½ teaspoon pepper and the eggs and blend well (there will be 3 generous cups filling). Bring 4 to 6 quarts water to boil in large pot while preparing sauce. Melt the remaining 8 tablespoons butter in a large saucepan. Add flour and cook, stirring until well blended and bubbly, about 2 to 3 minutes. Gradually whisk in the milk and heavy cream; whisk over low to medium heat until the sauce thickens and comes to a boil. Stir in 1 teaspoon salt, Sherry and nutmeg. Evenly spread about 1½ cups sauce on the bottom of a buttered 13×9×2-inch baking pan. Add 1 to 2 tablespoons salt to the pot of boiling water. Gradually add the manicotti noodles; cover. When water returns to boil remove cover and cook until noodles are just barely tender, 5 to 6 minutes; do not overcook (noodles will be cooked further when baked and may split open if overcooked). Drain noodles in colander, handling gently. Rinse with cold water and drain again. Fill each manicotti with ¼ cup chicken-mushroom filling, using fingers, knife or a teaspoon. Arrange filled noodles in a single layer in the prepared pan. Cover evenly with remaining sauce, about 2½ cups. Sprinkle with Parmesan cheese, then almonds. Bake in a preheated 375°F oven until top is lightly browned and

sauce is bubbly in the center, about 40 minutes. Let stand for a few minutes before serving. Remove noodles from pan using wide spatula; serve on heated plates.

Note: If desired, omit purchased manicotti noodles and prepare homemade noodles as in Cannelloni alla Nerone using recipe for Basic Two-Egg Pasta (see page 119). Fill pasta squares using a slightly rounded packed tablespoon chicken-mushroom filling. Fill and shape as for Cannelloni alla Nerone. Arrange filled noodles seam side down in prepared pan and proceed as above.

CHICKEN TETRAZZINI

A purely American dish, named after the famous, portly and wonderful Italian singer Luisa Tetrazzini. I imagine that it must have been created for her when she was on tour in the U.S., but where and by whom, alas, I do not know. In an emergency, the dish can be made from kitchen staples. It really is that old American favorite, Chicken à la King, baked with spaghetti.

6 SERVINGS

6 tablespoons (¾ stick) butter
8 ounces mushrooms, thinly sliced or 1 cup canned sliced mushrooms, drained
1 small sweet green pepper, seeded and cut into strips
⅓ cup chopped canned drained pimiento
3 tablespoons flour
2 teaspoons salt
½ teaspoon freshly ground pepper
⅛ teaspoon ground nutmeg
2½ cups half-and-half, light cream, or equal parts milk and heavy cream
¼ cup dry Sherry
3 cups diced cooked chicken, preferably white meat
2 egg yolks beaten with 2 tablespoons cream or milk
8 ounces thin spaghetti, freshly cooked not quite al dente and drained
½ cup freshly grated Parmesan cheese

Melt 4 tablespoons of the butter in a heavy saucepan. Add mushrooms, green pepper and pimiento and cook over medium heat, stirring constantly, for about 3 minutes or until soft but not brown. Blend in flour, salt, pepper, and nutmeg and cook for 2 more minutes, stirring constantly. Add half-and-half and cook over low heat, stirring all the while, until smooth and thickened. Stir in the Sherry and add the chicken. Remove from the heat and stir in the egg yolk mixture. Turn spaghetti into a generously buttered 3-quart baking dish. Spoon chicken mixture over spaghetti. Sprinkle with Parmesan and dot with remaining butter. Bake in a preheated 350°F oven for about 20 to 30 minutes or until thoroughly heated and golden brown; if you wish, run the baking dish quickly under the broiler to brown further. Serve hot.

Church Supper Chicken, Noodle, and Spinach Casserole

8 SERVINGS

2 frying chickens (3 pounds each), cut into pieces
4 cups chicken bouillon
¼ cup (½ stick) butter
¼ cup flour
1 cup light cream or half-and-half
Salt
Freshly ground pepper
1 teaspoon freshly grated nutmeg
3 packages (10 ounces each) frozen chopped spinach, cooked and squeezed dry
8 ounces wide noodles, freshly cooked al dente and drained
1½ cups tomato sauce
3 tablespoons minced green onion or chives
¾ cups freshly grated Parmesan, Romano or Swiss cheese

Combine chicken and bouillon in a large kettle and bring to boil over high heat. Reduce heat, skim, cover and simmer over low heat for 20 minutes or until the chicken is cooked through. Drain into a bowl and reserve chicken. Remove any fat from the broth; if possible, chill the broth in the freezer until all the fat has risen to the surface and can be easily removed. Cool chicken. Discard skin, fat and bones and cut meat into bite-size pieces; reserve. Return defatted broth to high heat and reduce to about 2 cups.

Melt the butter in a large saucepan over medium-low heat. Stir in the flour and cook for about 2 minutes. Stir in the chicken broth and cook over low heat, stirring constantly, until the sauce is thick and smooth. Blend in the cream. Cover the sauce and cook over lowest possible heat (preferably on a flame guard) for about 15 minutes to remove any raw flour taste. Season with salt, pepper and nutmeg.

Combine ¾ cup of the cream sauce with the spinach and spread over the bottom of a buttered 13×9-inch baking dish. Spread the noodles over the spinach, top with tomato sauce and sprinkle with green onions. Arrange the chicken pieces on the noodles. Top with the remaining cream sauce and sprinkle with grated cheese. Bake in a preheated 350°F oven until golden brown and bubbly, about 20 to 30 minutes.

Note: The casserole can be assembled ahead of time, refrigerated (not frozen) and baked just before serving time.

MANICOTTI IMBOTTITI AL FORNO
Baked Stuffed Manicotti

8 SERVINGS

1 box (8 ounces) manicotti shells (14 shells)

FILLING

2 tablespoons (¼ stick) butter
3 medium whole boned skinned chicken breasts (about 1½ pounds), halved and trimmed of fat
3 tablespoons minced parsley
3 tablespoons minced green onion
1 tablespoon minced fresh sage
8 ounces chicken livers, trimmed
4 ounces prosciutto, cut into small pieces
¾ cup freshly grated Parmesan cheese
Salt
Freshly ground pepper

SAUCE

6 tablespoons (¾ stick) butter
½ cup flour
5 cups milk
1 cup heavy cream
1 tablespoon tomato paste
½ teaspoon freshly grated nutmeg
½ teaspoon (about) salt
Freshly ground pepper
¾ cup freshly grated Parmesan cheese
1 to 2 tablespoons butter (optional)
⅓ cup freshly grated Parmesan cheese (optional)

Cook manicotti in plenty of rapidly boiling salted water for 6 to 8 minutes or until barely al dente; do not overcook. Drain and rinse under cold running water until shells are cool. Arrange on a clean kitchen towel with sides not touching.

For filling: Melt the butter in a large deep frying pan. Add the chicken breasts and cook over medium heat, turning frequently, for about 12 to 15 minutes or until thoroughly cooked. Remove from the pan and reserve. Add the chicken livers to the pan and cook, stirring constantly, for 3 to 4 minutes. Combine the chicken breasts, livers and prosciutto in food processor and grind finely but do not liquefy. Turn into a bowl. Stir in the parsley, green onions, sage, and Parmesan cheese. Taste and adjust seasoning with salt and pepper. Stir with a wooden spoon until well mixed; reserve.

For sauce: Melt the butter in a heavy saucepan. Add the flour and cook over low heat, stirring constantly, for 2 to 3 minutes. Whisk in the milk and cook, whisking constantly, 5 to 8 minutes after the mixture begins to bubble to remove all raw flour taste. Add the cream, tomato paste, nutmeg, salt, and pepper and mix well. Cook for about 2 more minutes. Remove from heat.

To assemble: Add 1 cup of the sauce to the meat mixture and blend well. Stuff into cooked manicotti shells. Arrange the shells in one layer in a buttered 9×12-inch baking dish, preferably one that can go to the table. Pour the remaining sauce evenly over the stuffed shells. If desired, dot the surface with 1 to 2 tablespoons butter and sprinkle with ⅓ cup grated Parmesan. Bake in preheated 400°F oven for about 15 to 20 minutes or until lightly browned. Serve hot.

—— • • • ——

SAFFRON CHICKEN ON NOODLES

A recipe of Burmese origin.

MAKES ABOUT 4 CUPS SAUCE;
4 SERVINGS

3 medium whole boned skinned chicken breasts (about 1½ pounds), halved and trimmed of fat
¾ teaspoon salt, divided
¼ teaspoon freshly ground pepper
6 tablespoons oil, preferably peanut, divided
2 large onions, minced (2 cups)
1 large garlic clove, minced
2 tablespoons flour
1 cup chicken broth
1 small can (5.33 ounces) evaporated milk, undiluted
¼ teaspoon saffron threads, crumbled and soaked in 1 tablespoon boiling water for 10 minutes, or ⅛ teaspoon ground saffron
½ teaspoon minced fresh ginger
¼ teaspoon hot pepper sauce
8 ounces medium egg noodles, freshly cooked al dente and drained
Minced parsley (optional)

With kitchen shears cut chicken into ½-inch pieces. Toss the chicken pieces with ½ teaspoon salt and the pepper. In heavy large skillet heat 4 tablespoons oil. Add chicken and cook over medium-high heat about 8 minutes or just until chicken is tender, stirring occasionally and reducing heat if necessary. Transfer chicken and juices to bowl; reserve. In same skillet heat remaining 2 tablespoons oil. Add onion and garlic and cook over medium to medium-high heat, stirring occasionally, about 8 to 10 minutes or until onion is tender but not browned. Reduce heat to low, add flour and cook, stirring for about 2 minutes. Stir in the chicken broth, evaporated milk, soaked saffron with liquid, the cooked chicken and juices, ginger, hot pepper sauce and remaining ¼ teaspoon salt. Bring just to boiling point, then reduce heat to low and simmer uncovered about 10 minutes or until sauce thickens slightly and flavors are blended (4 cups). Serve over hot cooked noodles. Garnish with parsley, if desired.

——— · · · ———

SPAGHETTI ALLA CARUSO

Louis Diat, the late great chef of the old Ritz-Carlton Hotel in New York (and inventor of Vichyssoise soup), created this elaborate dish for the pasta-loving tenor Enrico Caruso—or so Mr. Diat told me many years ago. The recipe that follows, reproduced more or less verbatim, is by no means home cooking, but it can be made at home. Incidentally, in culinary language "Caruso" always indicates the presence of chicken livers.

5 TO 6 SERVINGS

2 onions, chopped
1 tablespoon butter
6 fresh tomatoes, peeled, finely chopped
1 cup beef or other good gravy
6 to 8 mushrooms, sliced
4 to 6 diced artichoke bottoms, fresh, canned
   or frozen (if frozen, thawed)
1 cup diced chicken livers
Olive oil
1 teaspoon chopped parsley
1 teaspoon salt
Freshly ground pepper
1 pound spaghetti
½ to 1 cup freshly grated Parmesan cheese

Brown onions in a saucepan with the butter; add tomatoes and gravy. Sauté mushrooms, artichoke bottoms and chicken livers in olive oil, mix them into the sauce, add the chopped parsley and correct the seasoning.

Cook the spaghetti in boiling salted water for 15 minutes. Drain and place in serving dish. Sprinkle with grated Parmesan cheese. Pour the sauce over the spaghetti and serve very hot. Pass more grated Parmesan separately.

Pasta with Vegetables

Eggplant, Tomato, and Green Pepper on Spaghettini

Flemish Carrots with Pine Nuts over Shell Pasta

Linguine with Broccoli

Macaroni Eggplant Casserole

Macaroni and Spinach Casserole

Noodle, Saffron, Zucchini, and Tomato Dish

Pasta alla Norma

Pasta with Artichoke Hearts

Pasta with Many Vegetables

Piquant Spaghetti with Peppers, Onion, and Tomato Sauce

Ratatouille Lasagne

Sirio Maccioni's Original Pasta Primavera

Sliced Mushrooms on Thin Noodles

Spinach-Cheese-Filled Lasagne

Stir-Fry Vegetables and Noodles

Super Quick Vegetable Pasta Orientale

Tomatoes à la Crème over Fettucine

Quick Summer Spaghetti

Peppers, Onions, and Tomatoes

EGGPLANT, TOMATO, AND GREEN PEPPER ON SPAGHETTINI

A Middle Eastern recipe. You can double it and use part of the dish cold as a first course salad served on lettuce leaves; or serve hot, by scrambling eggs in the heated leftover sauce and using it on more pasta. For added interest, fry the spaghettini lightly before dressing with the sauce.

MAKES ABOUT 3½ CUPS SAUCE;
4 TO 6 SERVINGS

2 medium eggplants (about 1½ pounds)
2 teaspoons salt
½ to ¾ cup olive oil
1 large onion, sliced
½ cup pine nuts (optional)
1 large sweet green pepper, seeded and thinly sliced
4 large ripe tomatoes, peeled and sliced, or 3 cups canned Italian style tomatoes with their juice
Salt (optional)
Freshly ground pepper
Juice of 1 lemon (optional)
12 to 16 ounces spaghettini, freshly cooked al dente and drained*

Wash the eggplants (do not peel) and cut them into ¼-inch slices. Transfer half of the slices to a colander and sprinkle with 1 teaspoon of the salt. Add remaining slices and sprinkle with the remaining salt. Place a plate over the eggplant and top with weight (several filled cans or the like). Stand in the sink or on a drainboard and let eggplant drain for 30 to 60 minutes (this will get rid of their bitter juices). Squeeze the slices as dry as you can with hands or a spoon; dry with paper towels.

Heat ½ cup of the olive oil in a deep large frying pan or shallow saucepan. Add the onion and pine nuts and cook, stirring constantly, until the onion is soft and both onion and nuts are turning golden. Add the eggplant slices and the green pepper and cook over low to medium heat for 10 to 15 minutes, turning slices occasionally (if too dry, add remaining ¼ cup olive oil). Add the tomatoes, salt if necessary (eggplants are already salted), and pepper. Simmer uncovered over low heat for 15 minutes to reduce juices, then cover and simmer for about 10 more minutes, stirring frequently (mixture must be soft and the eggplant slices should have lost their shape). Remove from heat and sprinkle lemon juice over the mixture. Turn onto cooked drained spaghettini in a heated serving dish, or cool in the pan and serve as a first course salad.

*Note: If you wish, before topping with eggplant mixture fry the spaghettini, cooked al dente, in 2 to 3 tablespoons olive oil in a deep frying pan until it is turning crisp.

• • •

FLEMISH CARROTS WITH PINE NUTS OVER SHELL PASTA

Suitable for a light first course or as a luncheon or supper dish.

3 TO 4 SERVINGS

8 medium carrots, cut into 1½ × ½-inch sticks
½ cup (1 stick) butter
¼ cup water
Salt
½ teaspoon sugar (optional)
½ cup heavy cream
3 egg yolks
2 tablespoons (¼ stick) butter, melted
2 teaspoons fresh lemon juice
Freshly ground pepper
8 ounces small shells, freshly cooked al dente and drained
⅔ cup toasted pine nuts
3 tablespoons minced parsley or chives

Place the carrots in a flameproof casserole that can go to the table and is big enough to hold all the ingredients. Add the butter, water, salt and sugar. Cover the casserole and bring to the boiling point, then reduce heat to low and cook covered until carrots are tender (cooking time varies according to their age) but still firm; do not overcook. Shake the casserole every 3 min-utes to prevent sticking. Beat together the heavy cream, egg yolks, and melted butter. Stir into carrots and cook for 2 more minutes. Remove from heat and stir in lemon juice and pepper to taste. Turn shells out into the carrots and add pine nuts and parsley. Toss and serve hot.

LINGUINE WITH BROCCOLI

This standard dish is made more interesting by the addition of pine nuts or walnuts.

MAKES ABOUT 3½ CUPS SAUCE;
4 TO 6 SERVINGS

1½ pounds broccoli
½ cup olive oil
2 to 4 garlic cloves, minced
1 can (28 ounces) Italian style tomatoes, drained (about 1⅓ cups)
Salt
Freshly ground pepper
½ cup pine nuts or chopped walnuts
1 tablespoon fresh lemon juice
8 ounces linguine or other long pasta, freshly cooked al dente and drained
2 tablespoons (¼ stick) butter
⅔ cup freshly grated Parmesan cheese

Trim and wash broccoli. Peel the stalks; keeping small florets whole, cut stalks and large florets into ¼-inch slices. Pat broccoli dry. Heat the olive oil in a deep large frying pan over medium-high heat. Add the garlic and cook for 2 minutes. Add broccoli and cook, stirring constantly, for about 3 minutes. Add tomatoes with salt and pepper to taste. Reduce heat to low, cover and simmer, stirring occasionally, for about 10 minutes. Mix in pine nuts and lemon juice and simmer covered for about 5 more minutes. Turn linguine into a heated serving dish; stir in the butter and toss. Sprinkle the pasta with Parmesan and add broccoli mixture. Serve very hot, tossing at the table.

• • •

MACARONI EGGPLANT CASSEROLE

4 SERVINGS

1 eggplant (¾ to 1 pound)
Olive oil
1 medium onion, sliced
3 cans (8 ounces each) tomato sauce
1 teaspoon dried basil
8 ounces elbow macaroni, freshly cooked not quite al dente and drained
⅔ cup freshly grated Parmesan cheese
12 ounces mozzarella, cut into thin slices

Trim and peel the eggplant; cut into crosswise slices. Heat 2 tablespoons olive oil in a deep large frying pan over medium heat. Add eggplant in batches and brown on both sides, turning once; add more olive oil as needed (but do not use too much, since eggplant absorbs oil easily). Drain fried slices on paper towels and reserve. If there is no oil left in the frying pan, add 1 tablespoon. Add the onion and cook, stirring constantly, for 3 to 5 minutes or until tender. Stir in the tomato sauce and basil, cover and simmer over low heat for 10 minutes. Spread half the macaroni over the bottom of a buttered 1½-quart baking dish. Top with half the eggplant-tomato sauce, sprinkle with half the Parmesan cheese and top with half of the mozzarella. Repeat layers in the same order. Bake in a preheated 350°F oven for about 25 minutes or until mozzarella is golden brown and melting. Serve hot.

• • •

MACARONI AND SPINACH CASSEROLE

A good side dish. You can substitute small shells, bowties or similar pasta, for elbow macaroni.

6 SERVINGS

½ cup (1 stick) butter
1 medium onion, minced
½ cup flour
5 cups milk
Salt
Freshly ground pepper
1 teaspoon dried thyme or dried fine herbs
¼ teaspoon ground nutmeg
2 eggs, beaten
1 pound elbow macaroni, freshly cooked not
  quite al dente and drained

2 packages (10 ounces each) frozen chopped
  spinach, cooked and squeezed dry
½ cup fine dry breadcrumbs blended with 2
  tablespoons (¼ stick) butter, melted

Melt the butter in a saucepan, add the onion and cook, stirring constantly, until tender; do not brown. Stir in flour and cook over low heat for 2 minutes, stirring constantly. Whisk in 4 cups of the milk, salt, pepper, thyme, and nutmeg and cook, whisking constantly, until smooth and thickened. Combine the remaining milk and eggs and stir into the sauce; remove from heat. In a generously buttered shallow 3-quart casserole spread half of the macaroni. Top with the spinach, half of the sauce and the remaining macaroni. Pour the remaining sauce over the macaroni and sprinkle with the buttered breadcrumbs. Bake in a preheated 350°F oven for 20 to 25 minutes or until golden brown and bubbly. Serve immediately.

• • •

Noodle, Saffron, Zucchini and Tomato Dish

Prepare as quickly as possible to avoid mushiness.

4 TO 5 SERVINGS

4 ounces medium Chinese noodles or thin egg noodles
5 tablespoons butter
1 cup heavy cream
¼ teaspoon ground saffron or crumbled saffron threads
2 tablespoons minced onion or shallots
1 pound zucchini, thinly sliced
¼ teaspoon dried thyme
Salt
Freshly ground pepper
3 medium-size ripe but firm tomatoes, cut into ⅛-inch slices, drained of excess juice
1 tablespoon minced fresh basil or mint
Freshly grated Parmesan cheese

Cook the noodles in plenty of boiling water according to package directions until barely al dente. Drain and toss with 2 tablespoons of the butter. Place the noodles in a smooth layer in the bottom of a generously buttered 2-quart heated serving dish; keep warm in a low oven. Simmer the cream in a heavy small saucepan over low heat until reduced by about ⅓. Stir in the saffron and mix well. Remove from heat. Melt the remaining 3 tablespoons butter in a saucepan or a deep large frying pan. Add the onion and cook, stirring constantly, until soft; do not brown. Add the zucchini and thyme and cook over high heat, stirring constantly, for about 2 minutes or until just beginning to soften; the zucchini must stay crisp. Stir in the saffron cream and cook over medium heat for 3 more minutes or until heated through. Taste and adjust seasoning with salt and pepper. Keep warm over very low heat. Arrange the tomato slices around the edge of the cooked noodles in the serving dish. Pile the zucchini and sauce on the tomatoes, so that about ⅓ of the sliced tomatoes is exposed. Sprinkle with the basil. Serve immediately; the heat of the pasta and zucchini will cook the tomatoes sufficiently to remove any raw taste. Toss at the table and pass Parmesan cheese separately.

Pasta alla Norma

This recipe comes from Catania, in Sicily—hometown of Vincenzo Bellini, the famous composer of the operas *Norma, I Puritani* and *La Sonnambula*. The people of Catania named this dish in his honor.

MAKES ABOUT 4 CUPS SAUCE;
6 SERVINGS

2 medium eggplants, (about 1 pound each)
2 tablespoons salt
11 tablespoons olive oil

5 salted anchovies or more if mild (optional)
1 large onion, chopped (about 1¼ cups)
2 large garlic cloves, minced
1 pound ripe plum tomatoes, peeled and
   chopped (about 8)
½ to 1 cup dry white wine
Salt (optional)
Freshly ground pepper
⅓ cup shredded fresh basil leaves or 1
   tablespoon dried
1 pound rigatoni or other short pasta
¾ cup freshly grated Pecorino cheese

Peel eggplants, leaving ½-inch strip of skin on each of four sides. Trim ends; cut eggplants into ½-inch slices. Layer slices in a colander and sprinkle each layer with salt. Cover with a plate and top with weight (a large can or the like). Set colander in the sink and let stand for 30 to 60 minutes to drain off the bitter juices. Press down with your hands to extract all possible liquid. Pat eggplant dry. Heat 3 tablespoons of the oil in a frying pan. Fry about one third of the eggplant slices until golden on both sides. Remove with slotted spoon and transfer to paper towels to drain. Add 2 more tablespoons oil to frying pan and fry another third of the eggplant slices. Remove and drain. Add 2 more tablespoons of oil and fry the remaining eggplant. Drain and reserve.

Place the anchovies in lukewarm water to cover. Soak for 5 minutes; change the water and let stand for 10 more minutes to remove salt. As anchovies are soaking, heat remaining 4 tablespoons of oil in a saucepan. Add the onion and garlic and cook over medium heat, stirring constantly, until soft. Add tomatoes and bring to boil. Reduce heat and cook uncovered for 10 to 15 minutes, or until the sauce has thickened.

While the sauce is cooking, remove the skin and bones from the anchovies and chop them fine. Stir anchovies and fried eggplant slices into the sauce with a fork, mashing the eggplant into small pieces. Depending on the tomatoes, the sauce may be very thick; thin it with the wine to the consistency of pancake batter. Taste and, if necessary, add a little more salt. Add a generous amount of pepper and stir in the basil leaves.

While the sauce is cooking, bring a large quantity of salted water to boil. Cook the pasta al dente and drain.

Pour the sauce into a heated serving dish and add the pasta. Toss and sprinkle with the Pecorino. Toss again at the table.

If you prefer, combine the sauce and pasta in an 8- to 10-cup lightly oiled baking dish. Stir in half of the Pecorino; sprinkle the remaining cheese on top. Bake for 15 minutes in a preheated 400°F oven to amalgamate the pasta and sauce.

· · ·

PASTA WITH ARTICHOKE HEARTS

MAKES ABOUT 3 CUPS SAUCE;
4 TO 6 SERVINGS

2 packages (9 ounces each) frozen artichoke hearts, partially thawed and separated
½ cup water
½ teaspoon salt
6 slices bacon
2 tablespoons (¼ stick) butter
½ cup diagonally sliced green onions with part tops (about 8 medium)
1 cup heavy cream
½ cup freshly grated Parmesan cheese
¼ cup minced parsley
Freshly ground pepper
8 ounces spaghetti, freshly cooked al dente and drained
Freshly grated Parmesan cheese

In heavy large saucepan bring artichoke hearts, water and salt to boil over high heat. Reduce the heat, cover and simmer about 5 minutes or just until artichokes are tender. Drain well; set aside. In a large frying pan cook the bacon until crisp. Drain on paper towels. When cool enough to handle, crumble the bacon; keep warm. Pour off all but 2 tablespoons bacon fat from the frying pan. Melt butter with fat remaining in pan, add the green onions and cook over medium heat 3 to 5 minutes or until tender, stirring occasionally. Add the cream, ½ cup grated cheese, parsley, and ½ teaspoon pepper and stir over low heat just until heated through. Add drained artichoke hearts and heat through. Toss mixture with hot spaghetti. Turn onto heated platter and top with crumbled bacon. Serve immediately with additional cheese and freshly ground pepper.

VARIATION:
Pasta with Asparagus: Using frozen asparagus: substitute 2 packages (10 ounces each) frozen asparagus, partially thawed, separated, and cut into 1½- to 2-inch diagonal pieces. Cook asparagus until tender, 3 to 5 minutes; drain very well. Proceed as above.

Using fresh asparagus: Trim and peel about 2 pounds fresh asparagus. Cut stalks into 1½-inch diagonal pieces (you should have about 4 cups). Cook in small amount of boiling salted water about 5 minutes or until tender; drain. Proceed as for Pasta with Artichoke Hearts.

PASTA WITH MANY VEGETABLES

The selection of vegetables is based upon one's taste and what is available. Most of the vegetables should be cut into ¾-inch pieces and cooked quickly over medium to high heat to stay crisp. Depending on their original texture, some of the vegetables will be crisper than others, which makes for a good contrast. This recipe can easily be doubled or tripled. It is best to use open-end pasta to which the vegetables can cling.

MAKES ABOUT 6 CUPS SAUCE;
4 TO 6 SERVINGS

½ cup olive oil
1 medium onion, chopped (about ½ cup)
1 garlic clove, minced
½ cup minced parsley
1 leek, thickly sliced (about 1 cup)
1 medium-size sweet red pepper, seeded and chopped (about ¾ cup)
1 medium carrot, chopped (about ½ cup)
1 celery rib, chopped, (about ½ cup)
1 large artichoke, sliced*
1 turnip, chopped (about ½ cup)
4 large red radishes, thickly sliced
1 zucchini, sliced (about 1 cup)
¾ cup shelled peas
4 ounces mushrooms, cut into quarters
1 cup tomato sauce
Salt
Freshly ground pepper
1 teaspoon dried basil, thyme, or other herb to taste
12 ounces wheels, shells, elbows, penne or small rigatoni, freshly cooked al dente and drained
2 to 4 tablespoons butter
Freshly grated Parmesan or Romano cheese

Cook vegetables in the order given. For softer vegetables, cook to desired tenderness. Heat the oil in a heavy large saucepan over medium heat. Add onion, garlic and parsley and cook, stirring constantly, for 3 to 4 minutes. Add leek, red pepper, carrot, celery, artichoke, turnip, and radishes and cook over high heat, stirring constantly, for 3 to 4 minutes. Add zucchini, peas, mushrooms and tomato sauce and cook for 3 to 4 more minutes. Season with salt and pepper; stir in herb. Turn cooked pasta into a heated serving dish. Add vegetables and butter. Toss to mix and serve immediately, with grated Parmesan on the side.

*To slice the artichoke: Remove all tough outer leaves. Cut off about ⅓ of the top of the remaining leaves, keeping only the white-green part. Cut stem off flush with the base; trim base. Cut artichoke into quarters and cut out inner fuzz as you would core an apple. Slice thinly and drop slices into water with lemon juice or vinegar (3 tablespoons to 1 quart water) to keep from discoloring; drain before using.

——— · · · ———

PIQUANT SPAGHETTI WITH PEPPERS, ONION AND TOMATO SAUCE

If you have any leftover sauce, try scrambling some eggs in it for lunch or supper. A mixture of red and green peppers makes for a prettier dish.

MAKES ABOUT 6 CUPS SAUCE;
4 TO 6 SERVINGS

¼ cup olive oil
3 large onions, thinly sliced
3 cups drained canned Italian style tomatoes or 1½ to 2 pounds ripe plum tomatoes, seeded and chopped
6 medium-size sweet red and/or green peppers, seeded and cut into thin 2-inch strips
1 tablespoon dried basil or ¼ cup chopped fresh basil leaves
⅔ cup pitted Italian, Greek or other piquant olives, chopped
¼ cup drained capers (if very large, chop)
Salt
Freshly ground pepper
1 pound spaghetti, freshly cooked al dente and drained
Freshly grated Parmesan cheese

Heat the oil in a large saucepan or in a flame-proof casserole that will hold all the ingredients and can go to the table. Add the onions and cook over medium heat, stirring constantly, until soft but not brown. Add tomatoes and cook for 3 minutes. Add the peppers and basil and cook over low heat, stirring frequently, for about 15 minutes or until peppers are almost but not quite tender. Stir in olives and capers, cover and cook for 5 more minutes. Season with salt and pepper. Add freshly cooked and drained spaghetti to sauce, toss and serve with grated Parmesan on the side.

Note: For a sharper taste, add 2 to 4 drained anchovy fillets, minced, to the sauce.

——— · · · ———

RATATOUILLE LASAGNE

A good one-dish vegetarian meal.

MAKES ABOUT 8 CUPS SAUCE;
8 SERVINGS

2 small eggplants (about ¾ pound each), peeled, cut in eighths lengthwise, then cut into ¾-inch pieces
Salt
⅓ to ½ cup olive oil
4 medium-large onions, thinly sliced (4 cups)
4 medium-size sweet green peppers, cut into ½-inch pieces (2½ cups)
2 large garlic cloves, crushed

2 cans (28 ounces each) Italian style plum tomatoes, very well drained and cut up (about 2⅔ cups) or about 2⅔ cups peeled and chopped fresh tomatoes

3 small zucchini (½ pound each), cut in eighths lengthwise, then cut into ¾-inch pieces (6 cups)

1 cup minced parsley

¼ cup tomato paste

1 tablespoon dried basil

1 teaspoon freshly ground pepper or to taste

8 lasagne noodles (about 6 ounces)

1 tablespoon oil

1 pound mozzarella cheese, shredded

1 cup freshly grated Parmesan cheese, divided

1½ cups coarse fresh breadcrumbs, preferably from Italian bread

2 tablespoons (¼ stick) butter, melted

Place eggplant pieces in colander; sprinkle with 1½ teaspoons salt. Cover with a plate and top with weight (a large can or the like). Let stand at room temperature for 30 to 60 minutes to drain off bitter juices. Press down on eggplant to extract all possible liquid. Pat dry with paper towels. Heat ⅓ cup oil in Dutch oven or large kettle. Add onions, green peppers and garlic and cook over medium heat until onions and green peppers are tender, about 15 minutes. Stir in eggplant, tomatoes, zucchini, parsley, tomato paste, basil, 1 teaspoon salt, and ground pepper. Bring to boil over medium heat, then reduce heat,

cover and simmer, stirring frequently, about 1 hour or until vegetables are tender (you should have about 8 cups of sauce). If mixture looks too dry, add the remaining olive oil one tablespoon at a time. Remove from heat and set aside.

In large pot bring 3 quarts water to the boiling point. Add 1 tablespoon salt, then add lasagne noodles gradually so that the water continues to boil. Cook noodles about 5 to 7 minutes, or until al dente, stirring once or twice: do not overcook. Drain noodles, rinse in cold water and drain well. Return noodles to pot. Carefully toss with 1 tablespoon oil to prevent the noodles from sticking. Line bottom of buttered 13×9×2-inch baking pan with 4 lasagne noodles, cutting one noodle as necessary so that bottom is completely covered. Spread evenly with one-half of the vegetable mixture (4 cups). Sprinkle evenly with one-half the mozzarella cheese (about 2 cups). Sprinkle on ½ cup Parmesan cheese. Top with remaining 4 noodles, cutting 1 noodle as above so that cheeses are completely covered. Evenly spread on the remaining vegetable mixture; sprinkle with the remaining mozzarella. Combine remaining ½ cup Parmesan cheese, the breadcrumbs and butter in small bowl; mix well. Sprinkle breadcrumb mixture evenly onto the mozzarella. Bake in a preheated 350°F oven about 50 minutes, or until lasagne is hot and bubbly and crumbs are nicely browned. Remove from oven; let stand 15 minutes. Cut in squares and serve on heated plates.

SIRIO MACCIONI'S ORIGINAL PASTA PRIMAVERA

This is the one and true original that has inspired so many feeble imitations calling any pasta with a vegetable or two "Primavera." It originated in New York's great restaurant Le Cirque, where Chef Jean Vergnes refined the dish under owner Sirio Maccioni's tutelage. The glory of Pasta Primavera is its many fresh vegetables, properly prepared and quickly assembled. Admittedly, for the average home cook Sirio Maccioni's Pasta Primavera may seem quite a production—but it is not difficult, and it is wonderfully worthwhile.

6 SERVINGS

1½ cups broccoli florets
1½ cups baby snow peas (if snow peas are large, cut into halves)
6 medium asparagus stalks, peeled and cut into 1½-inch slices
1 cup fresh peas
1 cup zucchini, thinly sliced on the diagonal
1 pound spaghetti (preferably a good imported Italian brand)
3 tablespoons olive oil
12 cherry tomatoes, halved
2 teaspoons minced garlic
Salt
Freshly ground pepper
¼ cup minced Italian (flat-leaf) parsley

⅓ cup pine nuts
10 large mushrooms, sliced
⅓ cup butter
½ cup freshly grated Parmesan cheese
1 cup heavy cream
⅓ cup minced fresh basil leaves or 1 tablespoon dried
⅓ cup chicken broth or as needed
Freshly grated Parmesan cheese

Blanch broccoli, snow peas, asparagus, fresh peas, and zucchini SEPARATELY in boiling salted water for 1 to 2 minutes. This is done by placing each vegetable into a small bowl, covering with lightly salted boiling water, letting it stand for 1 to 2 minutes and draining in a sieve. As each vegetable is blanched and drained, hold the sieve containing it quickly under cold running water; each vegetable must be refreshed SEPARATELY (all of this affects the final freshness and crispness of the dish). Set blanched and crisped vegetables aside. (This step can be done ahead; cover and refrigerate the vegetables for no more than 4 hours.)

Cook the pasta in plenty of rapidly boiling salted water until al dente. Drain and reserve.

While the pasta is cooking, heat 1 tablespoon of the oil in a large frying pan. Add the tomatoes, 1 teaspoon of the garlic, salt, pepper, and parsley and cook over medium heat, stirring constantly, for 3 to 4 minutes or just until the tomatoes are soft but still retain their shape. Remove from heat and set aside. Heat the remaining oil in another large frying pan or flat saucepan large enough to hold all the vegetables. Add the pine nuts and cook until just golden brown. Add the remaining 1 teaspoon garlic, the blanched vegetables and the mushrooms and simmer over low heat for 3 to 5 minutes or until heated through. Remove from heat and keep warm. Melt the butter in a saucepan large enough to hold all the vegetables and pasta. Stir in the Parmesan cheese, cream and basil and cook over low heat, stirring constantly, until the cheese is melted. Add the pasta and toss to coat thoroughly with the sauce. If the sauce is too thick, thin with chicken broth, adding 2 tablespoons at a time. Add about ⅓ of the vegetables to the pasta and toss again.

Check the seasoning; if necessary, add a little salt and pepper. Divide the pasta among 6 large heated soup plates or bowls. Spoon remaining vegetables over each serving. Top with the cherry tomatoes. Serve immediately, with more freshly grated Parmesan on the side.

—— · · · ——

SLICED MUSHROOMS ON THIN NOODLES

A delicate first course, served without Parmesan at my house—though don't let that deter you from serving your pasta with grated cheese if you like.

MAKES ABOUT 2 CUPS SAUCE; 4 SERVINGS

3 tablespoons olive oil
1 pound mushrooms, thickly sliced
1 garlic clove, minced
Salt
Freshly ground pepper
2 tablespoons (¼ stick) butter, cut into small pieces
4 anchovy fillets, drained and minced
2 tablespoons minced parsley
Juice of ½ lemon
8 ounces thin noodles, freshly cooked al dente and drained

Heat the oil in a deep large frying pan. Add the mushrooms and garlic and cook over high heat, stirring constantly, for about 5 minutes or until the mushrooms are golden but still firm. Add a little salt (cautiously; anchovies are salty) and pepper. Stir in butter, anchovies and parsley and cook over medium heat for 3 more minutes. Stir in lemon juice. Turn pasta into a heated serving dish and toss with the mushroom sauce. Serve hot.

SPINACH-CHEESE-FILLED LASAGNE

The noodles do not need to be precooked for this dish.

6 TO 8 SERVINGS

1 package (10 ounces) frozen chopped spinach, thawed and drained
1 container (15 ounces) ricotta cheese
1 cup freshly grated Parmesan cheese, divided
1 egg
¾ teaspoon salt
¼ teaspoon freshly ground pepper
2 jars (15½ ounces each) spaghetti sauce or Quick Tomato Sauce (recipe follows)
10 lasagne noodles (about 8 ounces), uncooked
8 ounces mozzarella cheese, shredded
1 cup water

With your hands squeeze the spinach as dry as possible. Combine the spinach, ricotta, ½ cup Parmesan, egg, salt, and pepper in a large bowl and mix thoroughly. Evenly spread ½ cup spaghetti sauce or ¼ cup Quick Tomato Sauce in greased 12×8×2-inch pan. Arrange 4 lasagne noodles lengthwise side-by-side at one end of pan; place 1 noodle crosswise to fill remaining space in pan, breaking off a little of end of noodle to make it fit. Spoon one-half of the spinach-cheese mixture (about 1¼ cups) in small dollops over noodles; spread carefully into thin even layer. Sprinkle evenly with half of mozzarella (about 1¼ cups). Carefully spread on 1½ cups spaghetti or Quick Tomato Sauce. Repeat layering, ending with spaghetti or tomato sauce. Sprinkle evenly with remaining ½ cup Parmesan. Run a metal spatula or knife around edges of the casserole. With a teaspoon, spoon water around the edges (don't worry if some of the water mixes with spaghetti sauce; not all of water will fit around edges). Cover casserole tightly with foil, crimping edges. Bake in a preheated 375°F oven for 1 hour and 15 minutes or until noodles are tender. Let stand 15 minutes, then cut into squares and serve hot.

QUICK TOMATO SAUCE
Makes about 3¼ cups

¼ cup (½ stick) butter
1 large onion, chopped (1 cup)
1 large garlic clove, minced
2 cans (8 ounces each) tomato sauce
1 can (6 ounces) tomato paste
Water to fill 6-ounce tomato paste can
1 teaspoon sugar
1 teaspoon dried basil
¼ teaspoon salt
¼ teaspoon freshly ground pepper

Melt butter in large saucepan. Add onion and garlic and cook over medium heat until onion is tender, about 8 minutes. Stir in tomato sauce, tomato paste, water, sugar, basil and seasonings and bring to boil. Simmer uncovered, stirring occasionally, until slightly thickened, about 20 minutes.

STIR-FRY VEGETABLES AND NOODLES

4 SERVINGS

1 tablespoon vegetable oil
4 medium carrots, cut into thin julienne strips
3 medium zucchini, cut into thin diagonal slices
4 green onions, minced
½ teaspoon ground ginger
1 garlic clove, minced
1 pound fresh bean sprouts, rinsed and drained
¼ cup soy sauce
¼ cup water
1 tablespoon cornstarch
1 to 2 teaspoons sesame oil (optional)
¼ teaspoon chili oil (optional)
½ medium cucumber, cut into thin julienne strips
5 to 6 ounces cellophane noodles (bean threads) or 8 ounces thin spaghetti, freshly cooked al dente and drained

Heat the oil in a wok or deep large frying pan, add carrot and stir-fry 2 minutes. Add zucchini, green onions, ginger and garlic, cover and cook over medium heat for 2 minutes. Add bean sprouts, cover and cook for 2 minutes. Combine the soy sauce and water; blend into cornstarch a little at a time. Stir into vegetables. Stir in sesame and chili oils and stir-fry until the sauce has thickened and vegetables are tender. Remove from heat and stir in cucumber. Serve over hot noodles or thin spaghetti.

SUPER QUICK VEGETABLE-PASTA ORIENTALE

Easily doubled, tripled or quadrupled—just buy several packages of Stir Fry Frozen Vegetables and use desired amounts of Chinese or Japanese noodles, thin egg noodles or transparent noodles.

MAKES ABOUT 1⅓ CUPS SAUCE; 2 SERVINGS

1 package (10 ounces) frozen Stir Fry Vegetables
1 cup thinly shredded cooked chicken or other cooked meat (optional)
4 to 6 ounces thin noodles, freshly cooked al dente and drained

Prepare Stir Fry Vegetables according to package directions. Add meat and cook 1 to 2 minutes longer or until heated through. Turn noodles into heated serving dish or individual plates and top with vegetables. Serve hot.

TOMATOES À LA CRÈME OVER FETTUCINE

MAKES 2 CUPS SAUCE;
4 SERVINGS

6 large firm-ripe tomatoes, unpeeled
3 tablespoons butter
Salt
¾ cup heavy cream
Freshly ground pepper
12 ounces medium fettucine or noodles,
　freshly cooked al dente and drained

Cut off a thin slice at each end of tomatoes, then halve the tomatoes crosswise. Melt the butter in a deep large frying pan. Add tomatoes, cut side down, and puncture the rounded side with the point of a knife in 2 or 3 places. Cook over medium heat for 4 to 5 minutes. Turn the tomatoes, sprinkle with salt and cook for 3 more minutes. Turn again to let the juices run out, then turn once more to bring cut side up. Pour in cream and blend with the pan juices. Taste and adjust seasoning with salt and pepper. When the sauce is bubbling and very hot, place the noodles on a heated serving dish and turn tomatoes and sauce over them. Serve hot.

QUICK SUMMER SPAGHETTI

This can be easily doubled, tripled or quadrupled.

MAKES ABOUT 3½ CUPS SAUCE;
2 TO 3 SERVINGS

2 medium to large cucumbers
2 large ripe tomatoes
⅓ cup olive oil
¼ cup mild red or white wine vinegar
1 tablespoon minced onion
1 teaspoon dried basil or 2 tablespoons minced
　fresh basil leaves
Salt
Freshly ground pepper
8 ounces spaghetti, freshly cooked al dente
　and drained
2 tablespoons minced parsley or chives

Peel cucumbers if they are waxed. Cut lengthwise into quarters and scrape out largest seeds. Cut into 1-inch pieces. If desired, peel tomatoes by dipping them quickly into boiling water and slipping off skin; chop into 1-inch pieces. Place in a serving bowl and mix. Combine oil, vinegar, onion, basil, salt and pepper and mix thoroughly. Pour over cucumbers and tomatoes. Add spaghetti and toss to mix. Sprinkle with parsley or chives. Serve warm or at room temperature.

Note: Salad and dressing may be prepared ahead of time, combined and refrigerated. Add cooked and drained spaghetti just before serving.

· · ·

PEPPERS, ONIONS AND TOMATOES

Versions of this dish are found from Rome on south, some with fewer peppers, some with fewer onions, others with olives, capers or anchovies added. They all taste good—hot or cold as an antipasto, a side dish, or to sauce a plate of hot spaghetti.

6 SERVINGS

¼ cup olive oil
3 large onions, thinly sliced
1 pound ripe tomatoes, seeded and chopped or 2 cups drained canned Italian style tomatoes
¼ cup minced fresh basil leaves or 1 tablespoon dried
Salt
Freshly ground pepper
6 medium-size sweet green or red peppers, cut into strips

Heat olive oil in a heavy large saucepan. Add onions and cook over medium heat, stirring constantly, for 3 to 4 minutes, or until onions are soft but not brown. Add tomatoes, basil, and salt and pepper to taste and cook uncovered over low heat for about 10 minutes. Add peppers, cover and simmer for 10 more minutes, or until the peppers are tender.

Homemade Pasta and Fillings

Basic Egg Pasta

Super Soft Egg Pasta

Beet Pasta

Buckwheat Pasta

Eggless Pasta

Spinach Pasta

Wholewheat Pasta

Chicken Filling

Sausage Filling

Spinach-Ricotta Filling

Chocolate Pasta In Sweet and Hot Sauce

Ravioli

Tortellini

WHAT YOU NEED TO MAKE PASTA

The first step in pasta making is to make sure that you have plenty of space to function in. You need a work surface that is the right height for you to mix and knead the dough; you may use a counter, table or a board set on a piece of furniture the right height. Avoid plastic or laminated surfaces because the dough will stick to them. Be sure also to keep your work surface clean by scraping it free of bits of sticky dough and keeping it lightly floured. You will also need room to set out your rolled out dough and the finished cut noodles or pasta. Empty a counter, cover the space with clean kitchen towels, flour them lightly and they will be ready to store your pasta while it is drying out and resting.

Your equipment is simple. You can mix the dough in a large bowl or directly on the work surface. To mix the dough, you need a fork and measuring cup and spoons. To roll the dough out, you need either a rolling pin or a pasta machine. The rolling pins used in Italy are long, thin ones, sold in this country as French rolling pins. You roll out more dough with such a long pin, but a regular rolling pin will also do very well. To cut the rolled out dough into noodle strips, either use the machine or a sharp knife. To dry out the ready noodles, either place them on the kitchen towels as described above, or drape the back of chairs with lightly floured kitchen towels and hang the noodles over them.

To cook the pasta, you will need a very large kettle (this is essential). Since you will have to fill it with water and lift it it is better not to choose a kettle that is very heavy in itself. To drain the pasta, a colander or a spoon-shaped pasta rake (the colander does just as well) completes the basic equipment. There are also any number of gadgets that promise you the world. Unless gadgets amuse you, they are not necessary for making excellent pasta.

BASIC EGG PASTA

ONE EGG

1 large egg
1 tablespoon water
1 teaspoon oil, preferably olive
¾ cup unbleached all purpose flour*
⅛ teaspoon salt
About ¼ cup unbleached all purpose flour for kneading, rolling and cutting

Makes about 6 ounces

TWO EGG

2 large eggs
2 tablespoons water
2 teaspoons oil, preferably olive
1½ cups unbleached all purpose flour
¼ teaspoon salt
About ½ cup unbleached all purpose flour for kneading, rolling and cutting

Makes about 12 ounces

THREE EGG

3 large eggs
3 tablespoons water
1 tablespoon oil, preferably olive
2¼ cups unbleached all purpose flour
⅜ teaspoon salt
About ¾ cup unbleached all purpose flour for kneading, rolling and cutting

Makes about 1 pound 2 ounces

FOUR EGG

4 large eggs
¼ cup water
4 teaspoons oil, preferably olive
3 cups unbleached all purpose flour
½ teaspoon salt
About 1 cup unbleached all purpose flour for kneading, rolling and cutting

Makes about 1½ pounds

The following pages illustrate how to make pasta. (1) In large bowl beat the egg(s), water and oil with fork until well combined. Add flour and salt. Using circular motion, continue to mix until egg and flour mixtures are well combined, scraping sides of bowl with fork occasionally. Gather dough together using fork, hands or spatula. Sprinkle work surface with some of flour reserved for kneading, rolling and cutting and turn dough out onto floured surface and sprinkle lightly with some more of the flour. (2) Knead until dough is no longer sticky and a smooth elastic ball is formed, about 5 minutes; dough should have a firm bounce and velvety touch. Gently rub all sides of dough lightly with flour. Cover dough with a bowl and let rest at room temperature 15 minutes. (3) Cut into equal portions if preparing more than one Egg Pasta (Two Egg Pasta—2 portions; Three Egg Pasta—3 portions; Four Egg Pasta—4 portions).

*See pages 129 and 130

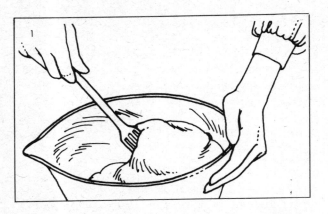

By hand: (4) Form one portion of dough into a ball. On lightly floured surface (use some of remaining flour reserved for kneading, rolling and cutting) flatten dough slightly with rolling pin. (5) Roll dough into a circle of even thickness, about 17 to 18 inches in diameter and about the thickness of a dime. As it is rolled turn circle frequently, occasionally flouring both bottom and top with enough flour to prevent dough from sticking to surface. Gently rub entire top of circle with flour. Pick up the edge of circle of dough farthest from you and loosely fold over about 2½ inches. Lightly flour top of folded section. (6) Continue folding dough toward you jelly-roll fashion, flouring top of each folded section, until entire circle has been folded into

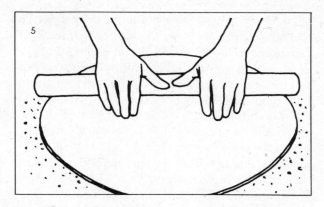

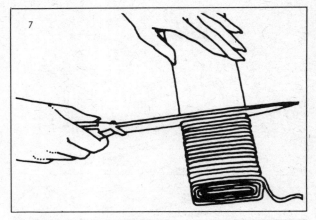

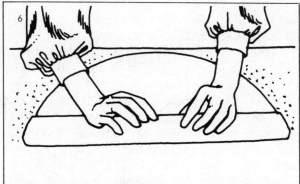

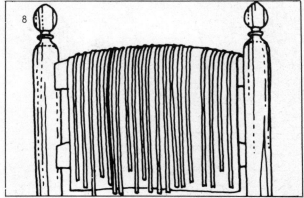

roll about 16 inches long and 2½ inches wide. (7) Using French or other large sharp knife, cut roll of dough crosswise into noodles of desired widths. Sprinkle folded noodles lightly with flour; toss very lightly to separate. (8) Hang noodles to dry side by side over waxed paper or clean towel hung over straight-back chairs, broom handle set across two chairs or on pasta drying rack. Or, if desired, spread noodles loosely on large towel-lined tray (or trays, depending on amount of noodles to be made), sprinkling with more flour if necessary to prevent sticking. If making more than one Egg Pasta repeat with each remaining portion of dough.

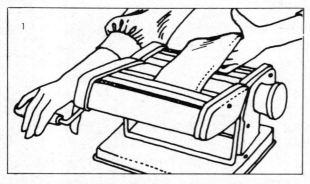

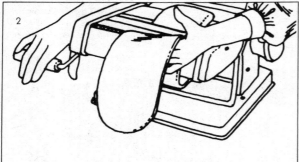

By machine: Working with one portion of dough at a time, rub both sides of dough with some of remaining flour reserved for kneading, rolling and cutting using slightly more flour for cut side. Flatten dough portion into about a 3×6-inch rectangle. Flour both sides lightly again. (1) Feed dough through widest roller setting of machine, placing narrow side at roller edge. Flour well both sides of extruded dough. Set rollers of machine one notch closer and again feed dough through machine, narrow side at roller edge. Each time dough is rolled through rollers take end gently with fingers and carefully pull dough out to full length without folding or stretching. (2) Repeat the rolling, setting the rollers closer each time and flouring only if dough is sticky, until dough is a long strip as thin as you want it. For fettucine and thin noodles, stop rolling at the next to last setting. For spaghetti, stop at the third to the last setting (since machines differ, you may want to stop at a setting thicker or thinner). Cut strip crosswise into 12- to 15-inch lengths for easy handling. Lightly and evenly rub a little flour into both sides of strips, using slightly more flour if dough is to be cut into spaghetti. Using hand to drape dough, feed strips through medium wide blades for fettucine or through narrow blades for spaghetti, placing narrow side of strip at blade edge. (3) After about half of strip has been fed through blades, drape hand under noodles as cutting is continued and finally completed to keep noodles from falling to the surface. Hang or spread noodles to dry as for hand cut noodles. If making more than one Egg Pasta repeat with each remaining portion of dough.

Cooking: After all noodles have been cut, it's best to cook them right away. If not to be cooked immediately, you can allow noodles to dry until leathery but flexible (time will vary according to temperature and humidity). Then transfer noodles to airtight containers or plastic bags and refrigerate for as long as 2 days or freeze up to 2 months. Do not thaw frozen noodles before cooking. Or dry noodles thoroughly and store in airtight containers at room temperature, handling carefully—homemade noodles are very brittle when dried. For every 8 to 12 ounces of pasta, fresh or dried, bring 3 quarts water to rapid boil in large pot. Add 1 tablespoon salt; gradually add pasta. Cover just long enough to bring water to boil again. Remove cover and stir gently and briefly only if pasta needs to be separated. Boil uncovered until pasta is al dente or firm to the bite. (Test by using a fork to lift out a sample. Bite a piece; pasta should be flexible but slightly resistant. Cooking time will vary according to the type of flour used, whether pasta is fresh or dried, and its thickness, shape and size. Fresh pasta made with white flour, spinach or beets may take just 1 or 2 minutes. Firmer, thicker fresh pasta made with wholewheat or buckwheat flour may take 3 to 4 minutes.) Drain pasta. Turn into a heated serving dish and serve immediately, sauced as desired.

SUPER SOFT EGG PASTA

Silky, too soft for spaghetti.

8 TO 9 OUNCES

2 eggs
1 cup unbleached all purpose flour
⅛ teaspoon salt
½ cup unbleached all purpose flour for
    kneading, rolling and cutting

1 POUND 1 OUNCE

4 eggs
2 cups unbleached all purpose flour
¼ teaspoon salt
¾ cup unbleached all purpose flour for
    kneading, rolling and cutting

1 POUND 9 OUNCES

6 eggs
3 cups unbleached all purpose flour
⅜ teaspoon flour
1 cup unbleached all purpose flour for
    kneading, rolling and cutting

In a large bowl beat eggs well with a fork. Add flour and salt. Using circular motion, mix well with fork until egg and flour mixtures are well combined, scraping sides of bowl with fork occasionally. Gather dough together (dough will be very sticky) using fork or spatula. Sprinkle work surface with some of flour reserved for kneading and cutting. Turn dough out onto floured surface. Sprinkle with some more flour. Knead using enough additional reserved flour until dough is no longer sticky and a smooth elastic ball is formed, about 5 minutes. Dough should have a firm bounce and velvety touch. Gently rub all sides of dough lightly with flour. Cover dough with a bowl and let rest at room temperature 15 minutes. Cut into equal portions (8 to 9 ounces—2 portions; 17 ounces—4 portions; 25 ounces—6 portions). Using one portion of dough at a time proceed as for Basic Egg Pasta.

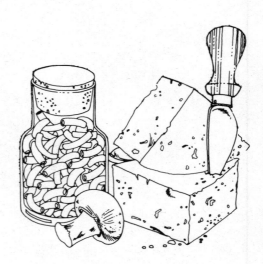

BEET PASTA

This is a very soft dough, not recommended for spaghetti. The beet has a greater effect on color than on flavor.

ONE EGG

1 large egg
1 tablespoon water
1 tablespoon strained cooked beet (see Note)
¾ cup unbleached all purpose flour
⅛ teaspoon salt
About ⅓ cup unbleached all purpose flour for kneading, rolling and cutting

Makes about 6 ounces

TWO EGG

2 large eggs
2 tablespoons water
2 tablespoons strained cooked beet (see Note)
1½ cups unbleached all purpose flour
¼ teaspoon salt
About ½ cup unbleached all purpose flour for kneading, rolling and cutting

Makes about 12 ounces

THREE EGG

3 large eggs
3 tablespoons water
3 tablespoons strained cooked beet (see Note)
2¼ cups unbleached all purpose flour
⅜ teaspoon salt
About ¾ cup unbleached all purpose flour for kneading, rolling and cutting

Makes about 1 pound 2 ounces

FOUR EGG

4 large eggs
¼ cup water
¼ cup strained cooked beet (see Note)
3 cups unbleached all purpose flour
½ teaspoon salt
About 1 cup unbleached all purpose flour for kneading, rolling and cutting

Makes about 1½ pounds

In a large bowl beat the egg(s), water and beet with fork until well combined. Add flour and salt. Using circular motion with fork mix until well combined, scraping sides of bowl with fork occasionally. Proceed as for Basic Egg Pasta.

To prepare beets: Using 2 medium-small beets, cut off any tops about 1 to 2 inches from the crown. Wash beets well, using scrub brush if necessary. Cook whole and unpeeled in boiling salted water to cover until tender, 15 minutes to 1 hour depending on age and size of beets. Drain. Cool under cold running water. Trim crown and root ends and rub off skin. Cut beets into small pieces, then rub through a medium fine strainer. Makes about ¼ cup.

BUCKWHEAT PASTA

A tender, somewhat gritty dough, which lacks some of the elasticity of Basic Egg Pasta. Best for noodles; not recommended for spaghetti. Since the dough thins out very fast, machine rolling through the first three notches is recommended. Do not be concerned if, in machine rolling, the edges of the strips crack slightly.

ONE EGG
1 large egg
1 tablespoon water
1 teaspoon oil, preferably olive
½ cup buckwheat flour
¼ cup unbleached all-purpose flour
⅛ teaspoon salt
About ¼ cup unbleached all purpose flour for kneading, rolling and cutting

Makes about 6 ounces

TWO EGG
2 large eggs
2 tablespoons water
2 teaspoons oil, preferably olive
1 cup buckwheat flour
½ cup unbleached all purpose flour
¼ teaspoon salt
About ½ cup unbleached all purpose flour for kneading, rolling and cutting

Makes about 12 ounces

THREE EGG
3 large eggs
3 tablespoons water
1 tablespoon oil, preferably olive
1½ cups buckwheat flour
¾ cup unbleached all purpose flour
⅜ teaspoon salt
About ¾ cup unbleached all purpose flour for kneading, rolling and cutting

Makes about 1 pound 2 ounces

FOUR EGG
4 large eggs
¼ cup water
4 teaspoons oil, preferably olive
2 cups buckwheat flour
1 cup unbleached all purpose flour
½ teaspoon salt
About 1 cup unbleached all purpose flour for kneading, rolling and cutting

Makes about 1½ pounds

In large bowl beat the egg(s), water and oil with a fork until well combined. Add buckwheat flour, unbleached flour and salt. Using circular motion with fork mix until well combined, scraping sides of bowl with fork occasionally. Gather dough together using fork, hands or spatula. Sprinkle work surface with some of flour reserved for kneading, rolling and cutting. Turn dough out onto floured surface. Sprinkle lightly with flour. Knead using enough additional flour until dough is no longer sticky and smooth elastic ball is formed, about 5 minutes. Dough should have a firm bounce and velvety touch. Gently rub all sides of dough lightly with flour. Cover dough with a bowl and let rest at room temperature 15 minutes. Cut into equal portions if preparing more than one Egg Pasta (two Egg Pasta—2 portions; three Egg Pasta—3 portions; four Egg Pasta—4 portions). Using one portion of dough at a time proceed as in basic egg pasta.

Note: If cutting pasta by machine, stop rolling at the third to last setting.

EGGLESS PASTA

This makes a soft, silky, smooth dough which stretches easily, best suited for noodles. To cut into spaghetti by machine, use very well floured strips of dough.

6 OUNCES
¼ cup water
¾ cup unbleached all purpose flour
¼ teaspoon salt
About ⅓ cup unbleached all purpose flour for kneading, rolling and cutting

12 OUNCES
½ cup water
1½ cups unbleached all purpose flour
½ teaspoon salt
About ½ cup unbleached all purpose flour for kneading, rolling and cutting

1 POUND 2 OUNCES
¾ cup water
2¼ cups unbleached all purpose flour
¾ teaspoon salt
About ¾ cup unbleached all purpose flour for kneading, rolling and cutting

1½ POUNDS
1 cup water
3 cups unbleached all purpose flour
1 teaspoon salt
About 1 cup unbleached all purpose flour for kneading, rolling and cutting

Pour water into large bowl. Add flour and salt. Using circular motion with fork mix until well combined, scraping sides of bowl with fork occasionally. Gather dough together. Sprinkle work surface with some of flour reserved for kneading, rolling and cutting. Turn dough out onto floured surface. Sprinkle with flour. Knead using enough additional flour until dough is no longer sticky and a smooth elastic ball is formed, about 5 minutes. Dough should have a firm bounce and velvety touch. Gently rub all sides of dough lightly with flour. Cover dough with bowl and let rest at room temperature 15 minutes. Cut into equal portions if preparing more than 6 ounces of pasta (12 ounces—2 portions; 1 pound 2 ounces—3 portions; 1½ pounds—4 portions). Proceed as for Basic Egg Pasta.

Note: If cutting pasta by machine, stop rolling at the third to last setting.

SPINACH PASTA

This is a very soft dough with a very mild spinach flavor; it is not recommended for spaghetti. The green color fades when the noodles are cooked.

ONE EGG
1 large egg
1 tablespoon water
1 tablespoon minced and squeezed dry cooked spinach
¾ cup unbleached all purpose flour
⅛ teaspoon salt
About ⅓ cup unbleached all purpose flour for kneading, rolling and cutting

Makes about 6 ounces

TWO EGG
2 large eggs
2 tablespoons water
2 tablespoons minced and squeezed dry cooked spinach (see Note)
1½ cups unbleached all purpose flour
¼ teaspoon salt
About ½ cup unbleached all purpose flour for kneading, rolling and cutting

Makes about 12 ounces

THREE EGG
3 large eggs
3 tablespoons water
3 tablespoons minced and squeezed dry cooked spinach (see Note)
2¼ cups unbleached all purpose flour
⅜ teaspoon salt
About ¾ cup unbleached all purpose flour for kneading, rolling and cutting

Makes about 1 pound 2 ounces

FOUR EGG
4 large eggs
¼ cup water
¼ cup minced and squeezed dry cooked spinach (see Note)
3 cups unbleached all purpose flour
½ teaspoon salt
About 1 cup unbleached all purpose flour for kneading, rolling and cutting

Makes about 1½ pounds

In a large bowl beat the egg(s), water and spinach with fork until well combined. Add flour and salt. Using circular motion, with fork, mix until well combined, scraping sides of bowl with fork occasionally. Proceed as for Basic Egg Pasta.

To prepare spinach: Trim off roots and tough stems. Cut large leaves in pieces. Wash spinach well; drain. Cover and cook 3 to 5 minutes in the water that clings to the leaves. Drain in a strainer, then squeeze dry by pressing the spinach with a spoon against the sides of the strainer. Squeeze very dry with hands; spinach must be completely rid of water.

2 ounces or about 2 cups loosely packed spinach with tender stems yields about 1 tablespoon minced very well drained spinach.

Note: Half of a 10 ounce package frozen chopped spinach, cooked, drained and squeezed very dry, equals about ¼ cup.

WHOLEWHEAT PASTA

Follow recipe for Basic Egg Pasta substituting regular wholewheat flour, preferably not stone ground, for unbleached all purpose flour. (Stone ground flour produces a somewhat gritty dough.)

Note: If dough should develop a few holes (particularly after first rolling through machine), simply patch by narrowly overlapping the edges of the tear. Seal with slightly moistened fingertips.

Since dough is firmer than dough for Basic Egg Pasta you will probably need little extra flour for kneading and cutting.

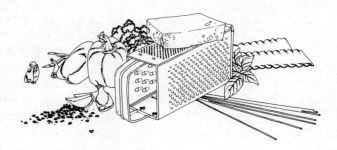

Pasta Made with Bleached All Purpose Flour

Follow recipe for Basic Egg Pasta substituting bleached for unbleached all purpose flour. Results are very acceptable.

Pasta Made with Semolina Flour*

Follow recipe for Basic Egg Pasta, substituting semolina flour for unbleached all purpose flour. The dough will have a rich eggy color and be beautifully silky and elastic. I prefer it to any other dough.

*Semolina flour can be found in specialty food stores and Italian or Mediterranean markets.

Chicken Filling

MAKES ABOUT 2¼ CUPS

2 medium boned skinned chicken breasts (about 1 pound), halved
1 teaspoon salt
¾ teaspoon freshly ground pepper
2 tablespoons (¼ stick) butter
2 tablespoons olive oil
½ cup minced onion
1 cup freshly grated Parmesan cheese
¼ cup minced parsley
2 eggs
¼ teaspoon freshly grated nutmeg

Remove all fat and gristle from chicken breasts; they should weigh about ¾ pound after trimming. Rinse breasts under cold running water, drain and pat dry with paper towels. Sprinkle the breasts on both sides with ½ teaspoon salt and ¼ teaspoon pepper. Heat 1 tablespoon each of butter and olive oil in a heavy large frying pan. Add the chicken and cook over medium heat for 5 minutes or until golden brown. Turn breasts and cook for 5 more minutes or until golden brown on second side. Reduce the heat to low and cook for 5 to 10 minutes, turning occasionally, or until juices run clear and chicken is tender (time depends on thickness of breasts). Drain on paper towels. Mince chicken or whirl in food processor; there will be about 2½ lightly spooned cups of minced chicken. Drain and clean the frying pan or use another.* Heat the remaining butter and oil. Add the onion and cook over medium heat, stirring frequently, for about 5 minutes; do not brown. In a bowl combine chicken, onion, cheese, parsley, the remaining salt and pepper, eggs and nutmeg. Mix thoroughly; this is best done with hands. Shape the filling into teaspoonful-size balls.

*The frying pan must be cleaned or changed after browning the chicken, or else the onions will turn brown and have tiny bits of meat clinging to them, turning the filling an unappealing brown color.

— · · · —

SAUSAGE FILLING

MAKES ABOUT 2 CUPS

1 package (13 grams) imported Italian dried mushrooms (optional)
1 pound sweet or hot Italian sausage (about 4 links), casings removed and meat coarsely chopped
1 tablespoon butter
1 tablespoon olive oil
¾ cup finely chopped onion
1 large garlic clove, minced
¼ cup tomato paste
¼ cup water or strained mushroom soaking liquid
½ teaspoon oregano
½ teaspoon dried basil
½ teaspoon freshly ground pepper
¼ teaspoon salt
½ cup freshly grated Parmesan cheese
¼ cup minced parsley
1 egg

Place the mushrooms into a strainer; wash thoroughly under cold running water. Turn mushrooms into a small bowl, cover with 1 cup lukewarm water and let soak for at least 2½ hours before using. Drain the mushrooms, reserving the liquid. Heat a heavy large frying pan. Add the sausage meat and cook over low to medium heat until browned, breaking up large pieces with a fork. Drain off fat and set the sausage aside. Heat the butter and oil in the same frying pan. Add the onion and garlic and cook over medium heat, stirring frequently, for about 5 minutes or until the onion is tender. Add the sausage, mushrooms, tomato paste, ¼ cup of the reserved mushroom liquid or water, oregano, basil, pepper and salt. Cook uncovered over low heat for about 15 minutes, stirring frequently, or until the flavors are blended (the mixture will be on the dry side). Whirl in a food processor or beat vigorously until the mixture is very fine—the finer the better—but do not let it become pasty. Turn into a bowl and stir in the cheese and parsley. When mixture has cooled, add the egg and mix thoroughly.

— · · · —

SPINACH-RICOTTA FILLING

MAKES ABOUT 2 CUPS

1 package (10 ounces) frozen chopped
   spinach, unthawed
¾ teaspoon salt
1 cup ricotta cheese, preferably whole milk
¼ cup freshly grated Parmesan cheese
½ teaspoon freshly ground pepper
1 egg yolk

Combine the frozen spinach and ¼ teaspoon of
the salt in a heavy saucepan, cover and cook
over low heat for about 20 minutes or until the
spinach is very tender. Turn the frozen spinach
frequently; when it has thawed, stir it frequently until it is cooked. Turn the spinach into a fine
strainer. With the back of a large spoon press
the spinach against the sides of the strainer to
extract as much liquid as possible. When the
spinach is cool enough to handle, squeeze it
very dry with your hands (there should be a
generous ½ cup). In a bowl, combine the spinach, ricotta and Parmesan cheese and beat in
the remaining salt, the pepper and the egg yolk.
Cover and refrigerate until needed.

CHOCOLATE PASTA IN A SWEET AND HOT SAUCE

This odd-sounding dish is a classic old recipe from
Tuscany revived by the greatest Italian chef of our
time—and famous cookbook author—Giuliano Bugialli. Bugialli is from Florence, a doctor of philosophy
and a wonderful sight to watch when he cooks. Get
his books for the real, historic food of Italy, presented
in a literate fashion.

5 CUPS SAUCE
6 SERVINGS

PASTA: (1½ POUNDS)
 1 recipe (1½ pounds) Four Egg Pasta (page
   119)
 4 level tablespoons unsweetened cocoa
   powder
SAUCE
 1 medium-size red onion
 3 celery ribs
 2 medium carrots
 1 garlic clove
10 sprigs Italian parsley
 ½ cup plus 2 tablespoons olive oil
 4 ounces pancetta (Italian bacon) or cooked
   ham, chopped
 1 pound lean ground beef
 1 cup dry red wine
 1 cup canned Italian-style plum tomatoes
Salt
Freshly ground pepper

¼ cup red wine vinegar
¼ cup raisins
2 tablespoons pine nuts
1 heaping tablespoon semisweet chocolate chips
1 tablespoon sugar

Prepare the pasta according to recipe directions but add the 4 level tablespoons unsweetened cocoa powder to the flour. The dough will be dark. Cut the dough into tagliatelle (or ⅜-inch wide noodles). Let the chocolate pasta rest on a pasta board, covered with a cotton kitchen towel, until needed.

To make the sauce: On a board, chop together very finely the onion, celery, carrots, garlic and parsley. Heat the olive oil in a large saucepan, preferably an enamel saucepan. Add the chopped vegetables and pancetta or ham and mix well. Cover over low heat, stirring frequently, for about 15 minutes or until tender. Add the ground beef and mix it with a wooden spoon into the other ingredients, breaking it up. Cook over low heat, stirring constantly, until the meat is browned. Add the wine. Cook until the wine has evaporated or for about 5 minutes.

Meanwhile, strain the tomatoes through a food mill or a strainer. Add the strained tomatoes to the meat mixture and blend well. Check the seasoning and add salt and pepper to taste. Over low heat, simmer without a cover for about 25 minutes, stirring occasionally.

To finish the sauce, combine the wine vinegar, raisins, pine nuts, chocolate chips and sugar in a small bowl. Let stand at room temperature for about 20 minutes. Then add the mixture to the meat mixture. Stir with a wooden spoon to mix well and simmer for 5 more minutes or until the sauce is thoroughly heated through.

While the sauce is cooking, bring a large kettle filled with water to a rolling boil.

When the sauce is ready, spoon about 1 cup of the sauce into a heated serving dish. Add the tagliatelle to the boiling water and cook for about 40 seconds to 1 minute. Do not overcook. Drain the tagliatelle immediately in a colander and place them in the serving dish lined at the bottom with the sauce. Spoon the remaining sauce over the pasta and toss thoroughly. Serve immediately, on heated plates.

Note: This sounds more complicated than it is. The trick is to have everything ready before cooking the tagliatelle, which are really done in seconds.

───────   · · ·   ───────

Ravioli

Remember that ravioli should be made as quickly as possible to prevent the dough from drying out. It is also important to have *neat* squares of dough; otherwise there may be filling caught between the sealed edges of the squares, which will cause it to seep out during cooking.

I like my ravioli with a thin dough and plenty of filling—both characteristic of the homemade product. Commercial ravioli have thicker dough and are filled less generously because such cost-cutting measures are commercially more viable.

MAKES 4 TO 5 DOZEN
1½-INCH SQUARE RAVIOLI

---

1 recipe Chicken Filling, Spinach Cheese
   Filling or Sausage Filling (page 131)
1 recipe Basic Two Egg Pasta (page 119)

Prepare filling and let cool completely. To speed up the filling process, shape filling into rounded teaspoonful-size balls before rolling out dough.

Prepare the Basic Two Egg Pasta according to directions. Let the dough rest for 15 minutes. (The dough may rest at room temperature up to 3 hours after kneading, as long as it is on a lightly floured surface and is covered with a bowl; or coat the dough lightly with flour and store airtight in a plastic bag. Do not let the dough dry out.) Cut the dough into 2 equal portions. Cover one portion of the dough with a bowl or store airtight in a plastic bag. Form the remaining portion of dough into a ball. Work the dough by hand or by machine as follows:

BY HAND

On a lightly floured surface roll out 1 portion of the dough into a strip measuring 27 to 30 inches in length and about 5½ inches wide. (The width of the strip at the ends will probably be somewhat uneven and narrower than the major part of the strip; the thickness of the dough should be uniform, and should measure about 1/16 inch. As the dough is rolled, turn it frequently, lightly flouring the bottom of the strip to prevent it from sticking to the work surface. When the dough is rolled out, carefully lift the strip and lay it down again without stretching it; this will help insure that dough is in a relaxed state and less likely to shrink when the filling is put on it.

With a fluted pastry wheel or the tip of a sharp knife cut off ends of strip so that the strip will be at least 4½ inches wide. What remains of the strip should measure about 20 to 25 inches in length and at least about 4½ inches in width. Cover the cut-off ends with a towel to keep them from drying out. Then, with a fluted pastry wheel or knife lightly score as many 1½-inch squares as possible; *do not actually cut through the dough.* (1) Place 1 ball of filling firmly in the center of each square. Alternatively, do not score the strip of dough, but place 1 ball of filling about every ¾ inches across and down dough strip. Cover the filled strip with a kitchen towel to prevent drying out.

Roll out the remaining dough to the same size as the first strip. Trim ends as for first strip. Lay over filling mounds, making sure they are entirely covered with dough. (2) With the narrow side of a spatula handle or with your index finger press down between filling mounds until the top layer of dough meets the bottom layer. (3) Using a fluted flour-dipped pastry wheel, roll the wheel between the ravioli, pressing firmly to cut through the dough, sealing 1½-inch squares. Separate the ravioli. With your fingers, pinch the edges of each square together very firmly to insure a tight seal; as you are doing this, flatten the filling mounds slightly with the tip of your finger. Ravioli will now measure about 1½ to 2 inches square.

In a single layer and without touching each other, place the ravioli on trays or baking sheets which have been lightly sprinkled with cornmeal to prevent sticking. Press all remaining scraps of dough together and roll into a strip measuring at least 4½ inches in width and ¹⁄₁₆ inch in thickness. Cut the strip in half; cover one half to prevent drying. Score, fill, and form ravioli as above.

BY MACHINE

Roll 1 portion of the dough with pasta machine according to directions on page 122, finishing with the second to last setting (the dough should be about 1/16 inch thick). The strip will measure about 27 to 30 inches in length and about 5½ inches in width; it will be somewhat uneven and narrower at both ends of the strip. (Measurements will vary slightly depending on the machine used.) Cut the dough about 20 to 25 inches long and at least 4½ inches in width; again, measurements may vary slightly. Score and fill as by hand; cover with a clean towel to prevent drying. Feed the remaining half of the dough through the machine and cut to measurements of first strip. Lay over filling and proceed to shape ravioli as by hand. Press the remaining scraps of dough firmly together, feed through machine to desired proportions, cut into halves, fill and finish ravioli.

STORING AND COOKING

Ravioli can be cooked right away, but it is preferable to let them stand at room temperature for 15 to 30 minutes to firm them up; or place in freezer and freeze partially.

To store ravioli in a box: Line a flat box with waxed paper and, if possible, sprinkle with a thin layer of cornmeal to prevent sticking. Arrange a single layer of firm ravioli on paper. Top with sheet of cardboard or waxed paper, sprinkle with cornmeal and make second layer of ravioli. Do not make more than 2 layers. Cover, seal and freeze up to 2 months.

To store in a plastic bag: Freeze ravioli partially. Pack loosely in an airtight plastic bag and sprinkle with a little cornmeal. Freeze up to 2 months. DO NOT THAW FROZEN RAVIOLI BEFORE COOKING.

To cook: Drop ravioli into a large kettle of rapidly boiling salted water. When the water returns to the boiling point, cook the ravioli about 8 to 10 minutes or until tender but not mushy, stirring frequently with a long-handled wooden spoon. Ravioli are cooked when filling is hot and dough is tender but still slightly firm to the bite or al dente; the best way of deciding if ravioli are cooked is to cut one open and taste. Cooking time depends on filling and on whether ravioli were fresh or frozen. Drain and serve with desired sauce on heated plates or in heated bowls.

Note: If you have any leftover filling, cover it and refrigerate. Use as filling for omelets or shape into patties and fry.

TORTELLINI

Making tortellini takes practice and patience. There are various ways of forming them, but I find the following size and method the easiest and most foolproof for occasional tortellini makers like myself.

MAKES ABOUT 11 DOZEN
¾-INCH TORTELLINI

1 recipe Chicken Filling, Spinach Cheese Filling or Sausage Filling (pages 131 and 132)
1 recipe Basic Two Egg Pasta (page 119)

Prepare filling and let cool completely. To speed up the filling process, shape filling into half-teaspoonful-size balls before rolling out dough.

Prepare Basic Two Egg Pasta according to directions. Let the dough rest for 15 minutes. (The dough may rest at room temperature up to 3 hours after kneading, as long as it is on a lightly floured surface and is covered with a bowl; or coat the dough lightly with flour and place in a plastic bag. Do not let the dough dry out.) Cut the dough into 2 equal portions. Cover 1 portion of the dough with a bowl or place in an airtight plastic bag. Form the remaining portion of dough into a ball. Work the dough by hand or by machine as follows:

BY HAND

On a lightly floured surface roll out 1 portion of the dough into a circle measuring about 15 inches in diameter and $1\frac{1}{16}$ inches in thickness. Cover ¾ of the circle with a clean kitchen towel to prevent drying out. (1) Using a 1½-inch round cutter, cut circles from the uncovered portion of dough. (2) Place ½ teaspoon of desired filling on the middle of the *lower* half of each circle. Bring the upper half of the circle over the filling and pinch the edges of the resulting half circle very firmly to seal in the filling. Flatten the filling slightly with the tip of your finger. (3) Draw the points together so they overlap; press firmly to seal.

In a single layer, arrange tortellini on trays or baking sheets which have been lightly sprinkled with cornmeal to prevent sticking. Press all the remaining scraps of dough together, roll out, cut circles and fill. Repeat with the second portion of dough.

BY MACHINE

Roll 1 portion of the dough with pasta machine according to directions on page 122, finishing with the second to last setting (dough should be about $\frac{1}{16}$ inch thick). Cut, fill and shape according to above directions. As scraps of dough are formed, keep them covered with a clean towel to prevent drying out. Press the scraps together firmly and re-roll; then cut, fill and shape. Repeat with the second portion of dough.

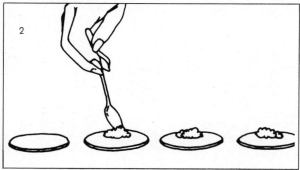

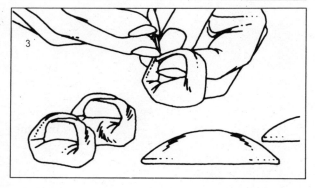

STORING AND COOLING
See page 123.

Note: If you have any leftover filling, cover it and refrigerate. Use as filling for omelets or shape into patties and fry.

Sauces

Anchovy Sauce

Creamy Mushroom Sauce

Flavored Butters

Gorgonzola Sauce

Marinara Sauce

Peas and Prosciutto Sauce

Pesto

Food Processor Pesto

Mortar and Pestle Pesto

Pirate Sauce

Pizzaiola Sauce

Saffron Cream Pea Sauce

Salsa Fría

Sauce Lamaze

Stracotto Meat Sauce

Tomato Sauce

White Clam Sauce

Zucchini Sauce

ANCHOVY SAUCE

This sauce can be adjusted to the desired degree of piquancy. Dress your pasta with it carefully; being on the sharp side, this will go further than a blander sauce.

MAKES GENEROUS ¾ CUP;
FOR 1 POUND SPAGHETTI

¼ cup olive oil
¼ cup (½ stick) butter
2 to 4 garlic cloves, minced
1 to 2 anchovies (2 ounces each), drained and
  minced or to taste
⅓ cup dry white wine
⅓ cup minced parsley
Freshly ground pepper

Heat olive oil and butter together in a small saucepan. Add garlic and cook over low heat, stirring constantly, until golden but not browned. Blend in anchovies and wine and cook over low heat, stirring constantly, until the anchovies have dissolved into the sauce. Stir in parsley and serve immediately over freshly cooked pasta.

— • • • —

CREAMY MUSHROOM SAUCE

MAKES ABOUT 2⅔ CUPS;
FOR 12 OUNCES EGG NOODLES

1 pound mushrooms
1 cup heavy cream
¼ cup (½ stick) butter
2 tablespoons minced shallots or onion
⅓ cup dry Sherry
¼ teaspoon mace
Salt
Freshly ground pepper
1 egg yolk
2 tablespoons minced parsley or chives
Freshly grated Parmesan cheese

Quickly wash and dry or wipe mushrooms clean. Trim and, if large, cut into halves or quarters; mushrooms should be chunky.

Pour heavy cream into a deep drying pan. Set over medium heat and boil gently until reduced by ⅓ or until cream is somewhat thickened, about 5 minutes; if cream threatens to boil over, remove from heat for a few seconds, then return to heat. While the cream is cooking down, melt 2 tablespoons of the butter in a saucepan or flameproof casserole that is large enough to hold all the ingredients and that can go to the table. Add shallots and cook, stirring constantly, until soft; do not brown. Add mushrooms and cook over high heat, stirring constantly, for about 2 to 3 minutes or until barely golden (the mushrooms must still be firm; if they reach the point of releasing their liquid the sauce will be too thin). Remove from heat and keep warm. Stir in Sherry, mace, salt and pepper and mix well. Whisk the egg yolk into the hot cream and add to the mushrooms. Keep hot but do not boil. Pour mushroom sauce, together with the 2 remaining tablespoons butter, over hot pasta; toss to mix and sprinkle with parsley. Serve immediately on heated plates.

——— · · · ———

FLAVORED BUTTERS

One of the glories of Italian pasta cooking is the pasta served "all'Inglese"—in the English manner (or so the Italians believe)—plainly dressed with fresh cold butter and plenty of freshly grated Parmesan cheese. Unadorned, however, the dish can get a little boring after a time. I find that flavored butters make for a welcome change of pace in what is the simplest and most practical pasta dish.

Flavored butters should be highly seasoned; if possible, use fresh herbs. The butters work best on long thin pasta such as spaghetti and fettucine. Depending on how rich a dish is wanted, a recipe using *one stick (½ cup) of butter will dress 4 to 6 ounces of pasta.*

The recipes here are easily doubled, but it is best to prepare them in one-stick batches. They can be prepared ahead and frozen; bring back to room tempera-

ture before dressing the pasta, or the pasta will be cold before the butter is completely melted. Serve with freshly grated Parmesan or Romano cheese.

SAGE BUTTER
Makes about ¾ cup

½ cup (1 stick) butter, at room temperature
2 tablespoons minced parsley
2 teaspoons grated onion
2 tablespoons minced fresh sage or 1½ teaspoons ground
Salt
Freshly ground pepper

Combine all the ingredients in a bowl or a food processor and blend thoroughly. Use immediately or turn into a freezer container, seal tightly and freeze.

CHIVE LEMON BUTTER
Makes about ¾ cup

½ cup (1 stick) butter, at room temperature
2 tablespoons minced parsley
¼ cup minced chives
1 tablespoon fresh lemon juice
Salt
Freshly ground pepper

Combine all the ingredients in a bowl or a food processor and blend thoroughly. Use immediately or turn into a freezer container, seal tight-

ANCHOVY GARLIC BUTTER
Makes about ¾ cup

½ cup (1 stick) butter, at room temperature
2 garlic cloves, minced or to taste
1 to 2 tablespoons anchovy paste or to taste
Salt (optional)
Freshly ground pepper

Combine all the ingredients in a bowl or food processor and blend thoroughly. Use immediately or turn into a freezer container, seal tightly and freeze.

GORGONZOLA SAUCE

In this dish pasta and sauce must be ready at the same time. Make the sauce while the pasta cooks, but start the pasta cooking first of all. I use penne for this, but any medium-size open-ended pasta will do.

MAKES ABOUT 2½ CUPS; FOR 12 OUNCES PASTA

3 tablespoons butter
8 ounces Gorgonzola cheese, cut into small pieces
¼ teaspoon sugar (only if cheese is very sharp)
1 cup heavy cream
Salt
Freshly ground pepper
Freshly grated Parmesan cheese (optional)

Melt the butter in a flameproof casserole that can go to the table and which is large enough to hold all the ingredients. Over very low heat, add the Gorgonzola gradually, stirring constantly to prevent sticking. If sugar is used, add it with the last pieces of cheese. As the cheese melts stir in ⅓ of the cream and cook, stirring constantly, about 3 to 4 minutes. Stir in another ⅓ cup of the cream; keep stirring but turn up the heat a little. When sauce has thickened slightly, returnr heat to very low. When the pasta is cooked al dente, drain it quickly and thoroughly and toss it in the casserole with the cheese sauce. Stir in the remaining cream and toss carefully to coat all the pasta. Season with salt (the cheese may be salty) and pepper. Turn up the heat slightly and cook, stirring carefully with a fork, for 2 to 4 minutes or until the cream sauce has thickened a little and the pasta has absorbed the sauce. Serve immediately, with grated Parmesan on the side.

Marinara Sauce

This is a tomato sauce from Naples. Like all popular indigenous dishes, people vary it, sometimes adding onion, wine or even sugar. What makes this different from other tomato sauces is that Marinara is thick and somewhat chunky, and that it is always flavored with garlic, oregano and hot red pepper. This sauce is best on heavy pastas such as rigatoni.

MAKES ABOUT 6 CUPS;
FOR 1½ POUNDS PASTA

⅔ cup olive oil
2 garlic cloves, minced
1 can (2 pounds 3 ounces) Italian style plum tomatoes, with their juice
1 can (6 ounces) tomato paste
1 cup dry red wine, water, or half wine/half water
Salt
Freshly ground pepper
2 teaspoons dried oregano or 1 to 2 tablespoons minced fresh
½ to 1 teaspoon crushed hot pepper flakes or to taste

Heat the oil in a heavy large saucepan, add the garlic and cook, stirring constantly, for about 2 minutes. Add all the remaining ingredients and bring to boil. Turn heat to low, cover and simmer for 30 to 60 minutes, stirring frequently. If sauce is too thick, add a little hot water or red wine, one tablespoon at a time; If too thin, remove cover and simmer until reduced to desired consistency.

PEAS AND PROSCIUTTO SAUCE FOR PASTA

The ham in this recipe must be full flavored. Odds and scraps from smoked hams can also be used.

MAKES ABOUT 5½ TO 6 CUPS SAUCE, FOR 12 TO 16 OUNCES PASTA

2 tablespoons (¼ stick) butter
2 tablespoons olive oil
⅓ cup minced onion
⅔ cup minced parsley
1 cup finely diced prosciutto or smoked ham, fat and lean parts
2 packages (10½ ounces each) frozen peas (about 4 cups)
¼ cup hot water, bouillon, or tomato sauce
½ to ¾ cup heavy cream
Salt
Freshly ground pepper
Freshly grated Parmesan or Romano cheese

Heat the butter and olive oil in a heavy saucepan. Add the onion and ⅓ cup of the parsley and cook over low heat, stirring frequently, until onion is soft but not brown. Add the prosciutto and cook 5 minutes longer. Add the frozen peas and hot water, cover and cook over low heat for about 10 minutes or until the peas are tender but not mushy. Stir in heavy cream. Taste and adjust seasoning with salt and add pepper. Simmer uncovered for 3 to 5 minutes or until sauce is heated through. Stir in the remaining parsley. Pour sauce over pasta and serve with the grated cheese on the side.

——— • • • ———

PESTO
(Basil Sauce)

This famous sauce from Genoa has now become an American favorite. It is used as a pasta sauce, or by the spoonful as an addition to soups, vegetables and even meats such as veal scaloppine. The basic flavor is fresh basil, and it *must be fresh*; the dried herb will not do. As in all classic recipes, there are any number of individual interpretations. You can use pine nuts, walnuts or both; add parsley to the basil, adjust the garlic to your taste, or use all Parmesan, all Romano or a mixture or, if you are a purist and can get it, only Sardinian pecorino (sheep's milk cheese). But on one thing all experts agree: *the olive oil must be of an excellent quality.*

Originally, pesto was made in a mortar, where the ingredients are crushed with a pestle (hence the name "pesto," which means mashed or crushed). That was before blenders and food processors, which also make excellent pesto; I personally make mine in a processor. Whether hand or machine made, pesto must be a mixture of ingredients chopped fine but not pureed, the consistency of thick pancake batter. Therefore, when using a blender or processor, use very brief on/off turns so as not to overprocess. Start with the smaller amount of olive oil, since the desired consistency may be reached before all the oil is used; it depends on how moist the herbs and nuts were to start with.

Serving Pesto: Here too, individuality prevails. If added to soups and vegetables, I serve the pesto by the tablespoonful as is, at room temperature. For pasta, I heat it somewhat, add about ⅓ cup heavy cream per cup of pesto and heat the mixture through, without boiling it. Some prefer to add 2 to 4 tablespoons room temperature butter for each cup of pesto, mixing the butter in until the pesto has absorbed it. Both cream and butter somewhat soften and enrich the rawish taste of the pesto. You can also add 1 to 2 tablespoons of the hot pasta water to the sauce to thin it a little. A rough guide to the amount of pesto to use: *before* adding cream or butter you should have about 2 tablespoons pesto for each serving. Toss it well with the pasta and serve in a heated dish. Pesto keeps well, which is fortunate since basil is a seasonal herb. It is eminently worthwhile to make pesto in large quantities for the basil-less months ahead, especially since it is so easily and quickly made in a food processor.

To preserve pesto: Place the finished pesto into a container with a tight fitting cover and pour a thin film of olive oil over the top. Close tightly and refrigerate (I keep mine for two to three weeks). Bring to room temperature before using.

To freeze pesto: For a fresher tasting pesto, freeze it without the cheeses and add the cheese to the thawed pesto. Work the cheese into the mixture before adding cream or butter. I confess that, to my shame (or so I've been chastised by purists), I freeze my pesto ready made to save time just before serving. However, I invariably add heavy cream to my pesto before serving it on pasta—not if I'm going to add it to vegetables or soups—and I've had no complaints. So please yourself as to how to freeze pesto. It will keep for three to five months frozen.

I find it more practical to freeze pesto in small quantities, from a maximum of 1 cup down to about ¼ cup. A large quantity of frozen pesto is a nuisance when you need only a small amount, and you can always thaw as much as you need. When I don't have the time to thaw the frozen pesto I simply put it in a saucepan and thaw it over VERY LOW heat before adding the cream.

When the top of frozen or preserved pesto darkens it means it has been exposed to the air. This doesn't matter; there is enough fresh green pesto under the dark layer to mix with and absorb it.

FOOD PROCESSOR PESTO

MAKES ABOUT 1 CUP;
FOR 4 OUNCES OF PASTA

2 cups loosely packed fresh basil leaves, no
  stems (if very large, tear into 2 or 3 pieces)
¼ cup pine nuts or walnuts, or 2 tablespoons
  each
2 garlic cloves, halved or to taste
4 tablespoons freshly grated Parmesan or
  Romano cheese or 2 tablespoons each
½ to ¾ cup olive oil
Salt (optional)
Freshly ground pepper (optional)

Combine basil, nuts, garlic, and cheese in food
processor fitted with steel knife. Process using
brief on/off turns until the ingredients are
chopped. Slowly pour the olive oil through the
feed tube, blending with on/off turns until the
consistency of a thick pancake batter; the ingredients should be minced but not pureed. Scrape
the sides of the bowl with a rubber spatula between turns. Check the seasoning; if necessary,
add salt and pepper.

MORTAR AND PESTLE PESTO

The proportions of ingredients vary slightly from
those of Processor Pesto because I found they work
better; my handmade pesto seems to absorb more
olive oil. Start with the lesser amount of oil and add
more until the basil and cheese mixture has reached
the consistency of a thick sauce.

MAKES ABOUT 1¼ CUPS;
FOR 6 OUNCES PASTA

2 cups loosely packed fresh basil leaves, no
  stems (if very large, tear into 2 or 3 pieces)
2 garlic cloves, halved or to taste
2 tablespoons pine nuts or broken walnuts
4 tablespoons freshly grated Parmesan or
  Romano cheese or 2 tablespoons each
½ to 1 cup olive oil
Salt
Freshly ground pepper

Combine the basil and garlic on a chopping
board and chop as fine as you can. Place the nuts
between 2 sheets of waxed paper or in a paper
bag and pound with a rolling pin or mallet. Add

nuts to basil mixture and chop again as fine as you can. Transfer the mixture to a mortar. Using the pestle, pound and grind it until the mixture begins to form a paste. Add the cheese and continue to pound and grind until mixture seems to hold together. Add the olive oil one tablespoon at a time, continuing to pound and grind until herbs, nuts, cheese and oil have combined into a sauce the consistency of thick pancake batter.

——— · · · ———

PIRATE SAUCE

I serve this piquant sauce with fettucine, but heavier pasta such as linguine, small rigatoni or elbows can also be used. The olives color the sauce a deep purple-red.

MAKES 2⅔ TO 3 CUPS;
FOR 1¾ TO 2 POUNDS PASTA

1 pound ripe plum tomatoes, chopped or 2 cans (28 ounces each) Italian style plum tomatoes, drained and chopped
¼ cup minced fresh basil leaves or 2 teaspoons dried
2 tablespoons (¼ stick) butter
2 tablespoons olive oil
4 anchovy fillets, drained and chopped or 2 tablespoons anchovy paste
1 large garlic clove, minced
½ cup chopped pitted black Italian or Greek olives
1 tablespoon drained capers
1 to 2 teaspoons minced hot red pepper or ½ teaspoon dried hot pepper flakes
¼ teaspoon oregano
Salt
Freshly ground pepper

Combine the tomatoes and basil in a saucepan. Bring to the boiling point, then reduce heat to low and cook uncovered for 7 to 10 minutes or until the tomatoes are soft. Push through a strainer or a foodmill or puree in processor or blender; reserve. Heat the butter and the oil in a heavy saucepan. Stir in anchovies and garlic. Over medium heat, blend garlic and anchovies into the butter-oil mixture with a wooden spoon to make a thin paste (this will take about 3 minutes). Stir in reserved tomato puree. Add olives, capers, hot pepper and oregano and mix well. Cover and simmer over low heat, stirring frequently, for 15 to 20 minutes. Taste and adjust the seasoning with salt and pepper. Serve immediately over freshly cooked pasta.

——— · · · ———

PIZZAIOLA TOMATO SAUCE

A chunky tomato sauce cooked just long enough to soften the tomatoes, so they don't lose their fresh taste. This sauce is served not only on pasta, but on steaks and other grilled meats and fish.

MAKES ABOUT 3½ CUPS;
FOR 12 OUNCES PASTA

¼ cup olive oil
2 pounds tomatoes, peeled, seeded and chopped
1 to 2 garlic cloves, minced
2 tablespoons minced parsley
1 teaspoon oregano
¼ teaspoon dried hot pepper flakes or to taste

Heat the olive oil in a saucepan and add all remaining ingredients. Cook over high heat, stirring frequently, for 5 minutes or until the tomatoes are soft.

Note: I have also made this sauce with 2 cans (28 ounces each) of *whole* well drained tomatoes. They're not as good as fresh, but the sauce is acceptable.

SAFFRON CREAM PEA SAUCE FOR THIN PASTA

Spaghettini, angels' hair, thin noodles and small to medium shapes like farfalle are suited to this sauce. The recipe can easily be doubled or tripled.

MAKES ABOUT 2⅓ CUPS;
FOR 8 OUNCES PASTA

1 cup heavy cream, at room temperature
⅛ teaspoon ground saffron or crumbled saffron threads
3 tablespoons butter
2 tablespoons minced onion or shallots
2 cups shelled peas (8 ounces) or 1 package (10 ounces) frozen peas
2 tablespoons water
¼ teaspoon dried thyme
Salt
Freshly ground pepper
1 teaspoon cornstarch dissolved in 2 tablespoons water (optional)
8 ounces thin pasta, freshly cooked al dente and drained
Sweet paprika or cayenne pepper

Stir together cream and saffron; reserve. Melt the butter in a flameproof casserole or large saucepan that can go to the table and that is large enough to hold all the ingredients. Add the onion and cook, stirring constantly, for 2 to 3 minutes or until soft; do not brown. Add the peas, water, and thyme, cover and simmer over low heat for 3 to 5 minutes or until peas are almost tender, stirring frequently to prevent scorching (if necessary, add a little more water 1 tablespoon at a time). Add the saffron cream and season with salt and pepper. Simmer uncovered for 5 more minutes or until peas are tender and the cream has thickened somewhat. If too thin, stir in cornstarch and cook, stirring constantly, until sauce has thickened. Add freshly cooked drained pasta and toss. Alternatively, turn into heated serving dish and sprinkle with sweet paprika or cayenne pepper to taste; the color will set off the dish. Serve hot.

· · ·

SALSA FRIA

A spicy Mexican sauce suited for pasta salads.

MAKES ABOUT 2 CUPS
FOR 4 OUNCES PASTA

1 pound ripe tomatoes, peeled, seeded and coarsely chopped or 1 can (1 pound) Italian style tomatoes, drained and chopped
1 medium onion, minced

1 medium-size sweet green or red pepper, seeded and minced
1 can (4 ounces) peeled hot green chilis, drained and minced or ¼ teaspoon crushed dried hot pepper flakes or to taste
3 tablespoons olive or vegetable oil
1 to 2 garlic cloves, minced
Juice of 1 large lemon or to taste
½ teaspoon oregano
Salt
Freshly ground pepper
4 ounces linguine, freshly cooked, drained and cooled

Combine all the ingredients except salt, pepper and pasta. Check the seasoning and add salt and pepper to taste. Chill well. At serving time, taste and adjust the seasoning once more. Turn cold linguine into a salad bowl. Add Salsa Fria and toss well. Serve immediately.

Note: The Salsa Fria may be made ahead of time and refrigerated. I find it best to keep the pasta separately and to mix it with the sauce only at serving time, to prevent the pasta from becoming soggy.

· · ·

Sauce Lamaze for Pasta Salads

This sauce was invented by the late and very great chef Albert Stockli, whose creations made the then newly opened Four Seasons Restaurant in New York celebrated throughout the world in the '60s. The recipe is to be found in Stockli's book *Splendid Fare* (Knopf, 1970), a crown jewel among cookbooks and well worth searching for since it is, according to the publisher, now out of print.

I use this sauce on macaroni salad as well as on seafood, poultry, and other cold salads. The only change I have made to the original recipe is to add ½ cup plain yogurt to the mayonnaise. I have kept the original wording of the recipe.

MAKES ABOUT 3 CUPS;
FOR 8 TO 12 OUNCES ELBOW MACARONI

In a mixing bowl blend thoroughly:
1½ cups mayonnaise
 ½ cup plain yogurt
 1 tablespoon prepared mustard
 1 tablespoon tomato ketchup
 ½ tablespoon chili sauce
 ½ teaspoon A-1 sauce

Then add the following:
 1 tablespoon finely chopped pimiento
 1 tablespoon finely chopped celery
 ½ tablespoon finely chopped chives
 ½ tablespoon seeded and finely chopped sweet green pepper
 ½ tablespoon finely chopped parsley
 1 hard cooked egg, finely chopped
 ½ tablespoon grated prepared horseradish

Blend all the ingredients and mix vigorously.

STRACOTTO MEAT SAUCE

Stracotto means overcooked in Italian, and overcooking is the secret of this sauce, one of the best in Italian cooking. The meat must be absolutely fat-free and the mushrooms the imported dry ones. Dry red wine may be used instead of Marsala, but Marsala imparts the best flavor.

MAKES ABOUT 3½ CUPS;
FOR 12 TO 16 OUNCES LONG PASTA

2 ounces imported dried mushrooms, washed and drained
1 pound boneless lean beef, such as London broil
½ cup (1 stick) butter
1 medium onion, minced
1 medium carrot, minced
½ celery rib, minced
½ cup minced parsley
1 cup dry Marsala
1 cup beef bouillon
Salt
Freshly ground pepper
2 tablespoons (¼ stick) butter or ⅓ cup heavy cream (optional)
2 teaspoons grated lemon peel

Crumble or snip the dried mushrooms into a bowl and soak in lukewarm water to cover for 20 minutes. Cut meat into smallest possible dice; do NOT grind it because ground meat gives a different flavor and texture to the sauce. Melt the butter in a heavy saucepan or Dutch oven. Add onion, carrot, celery and parsley and cook over medium heat, stirring constantly, for 3 to 5 minutes. Add meat and cook, stirring, until lightly browned. Add mushrooms and their strained liquid, Marsala and bouillon. Season with salt and pepper (bouillon may be salty). Cover tightly and simmer over lowest possible heat, preferably on a flame guard, for about 3 hours or until the meat has almost dissolved; stir occasionally. (The long cooking time is necessary to blend the flavors.) If after this time the sauce is still too liquid, remove cover and simmer for another 20 to 25 minutes until reduced to proper consistency. Stir in the 2 tablespoons butter or cream. Cook for 5 more minutes, then remove from heat. Stir in lemon peel for a fresh flavor. Serve over freshly cooked pasta or freeze.

· · ·

Tomato Sauce

If you want a very pure tomato sauce, make it with fresh tomatoes and only through step 1. If you proceed with step 2, you will still have a sauce that is quickly done and preserves the tomato flavor. Unlike the slow simmering tomato sauces from the Italian south this is the way the sauce is made in Tuscany, where it is called La Pomerola.

MAKES ABOUT 3½ CUPS;
FOR 1 lb. PASTA

3 pounds ripe plum tomatoes, halved or 3 cups drained canned plum tomatoes plus 1 cup of their juice
1 medium onion, halved
1 medium carrot, minced
1 celery rib, minced
2 to 3 tablespoons minced fresh basil leaves or 1 teaspoon dried
2 to 3 tablespoons minced parsley
Salt
Freshly ground pepper
⅓ cup olive oil

STEP 1

Combine the tomatoes, half of the onion, the carrot, celery, basil, parsley, salt and pepper in a heavy large saucepan. Bring quickly to the boiling point, then cook over high heat, stirring constantly, for about 5 minutes or until the tomatoes are soft. (Quick cooking preserves the fresh tomato flavor.) Puree through a food mill or sieve (a food processor will not remove tomato seeds and skins).

STEP 2

Mince the remaining onion half. Heat the olive oil in another saucepan, add the onion and cook until soft. Add the tomato puree. Check seasoning; if necessary, add salt and pepper. Cook uncovered over medium heat, stirring frequently, for 10 minutes or until thickened.

— • • • —

White Clam Sauce for Spaghetti

If you use fresh clams, use the liquid drained from the clams and round it out with bottled clam juice to the measure below. Don't forget to strain the fresh clam juice through a fine sieve lined with cheesecloth or a coffee filter to catch any fragments of shell and sand.

MAKES ABOUT 3¼ CUPS;
FOR 8 OUNCES PASTA

¼ cup olive oil
1 small onion, minced
1 to 2 garlic cloves, minced

2 tablespoons flour
2 cups bottled clam juice or liquid from canned clams and bottled juice
1½ to 2 cups minced fresh clams or 2 cans (10½ ounces each) minced clams, drained (reserve liquid)
½ teaspoon dried thyme, oregano, marjoram, or basil
Salt (optional)
Freshly ground pepper
¼ cup minced parsley
8 ounces linguine or thin spaghetti, freshly cooked al dente and drained

Heat the olive oil in a large saucepan, add the onion and garlic and cook, stirring constantly, until soft; do not brown. Stir in flour and cook for 1 more minute. Add clam juice and cook, stirring constantly, until smooth and thick. Add clams, thyme, salt if needed, and pepper; cover and simmer for 3 minutes. Turn hot pasta into a heated serving dish and add the parsley and clam sauce. Toss well and serve immediately.

ZUCCHINI SAUCE

MAKES ABOUT 6 CUPS;
FOR 1 POUND SPAGHETTI

¼ cup (½ stick) butter
1 tablespoon olive oil
½ cup minced onion
1 garlic clove, minced
⅓ cup minced sweet green or red pepper (optional)
4 large zucchini, sliced (about 2 pounds)
3 cups chopped peeled tomatoes or drained canned tomatoes, chopped
1 teaspoon dried thyme
Salt
Freshly ground pepper

Heat the butter and olive oil, add onion and garlic and cook over medium heat, stirring constantly, until golden and soft; do not burn. Add all the other ingredients. Cook covered over low heat for about 15 minutes, stirring frequently; the zucchini should be tender but still hold their shape.

MUSHROOM VARIATION

Makes about 7 cups; Sauté 4 ounces sliced mushrooms in 2 tablespoons (¼ stick) butter for about 2 minutes. Add to the sauce for the last 3 minutes of cooking.

Index

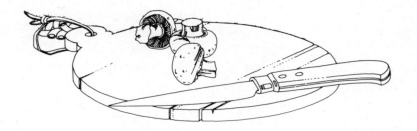

About the Author

Born in Rome, raised in Switzerland, and educated in England, Nika Hazelton has lived in the United States since 1935. She is the author of twenty widely acclaimed cookbooks and editor of *The Woman's Day Encyclopedia of Food*. Her food columns have appeared in nearly every major magazine, from *The New Yorker* to *Family Circle*. She is a former food critic for *The New York Times Book Review*.